CONTENTS

INTRODUCTION: HELPING YOU THRIVE ON "BLOWTORCH-ON-THE-BELLY" QUESTIONING

At some stage it happens to nearly all of us.

We're asked a question by the boss, a job selection board or a potential client – and we say something really stupid.

Or wrong.

Or self-defeating.

Maybe, on a bad day, it can even be a combination of all three.

And then you realize a short time afterwards what you should have said.

This human experience is so common, the French have an expression for it.

They talk about the annoying phenomenon of thinking up the perfect thing that should have come out of your lips all too late – while you're on the stairs leaving after that bruising verbal encounter: "L'espirit d'escalier", otherwise known as "the spirit of the stairs" or "staircase wit".

This book contains solutions to this and related problems.

It guides you on what you should say and how best to say it in challenging situations throughout your working life.

Whether you're asked "Why should you be promoted?", "Why aren't there any pens in the stationery cabinet when I asked you to get some last month?" or "Why should I invest in your billion-dollar project?", this book helps you formulate answers that are set to be more impressive, more reassuring and more inspiring than the ones you're giving now.

It gives you the techniques and the amazingly effective golden formulae for dealing with hard questions, nasty questions and stupid questions.

Drawing on my background as a broadcast interviewer, with training by the Australian Broadcasting Corporation in the art of putting business leaders, politicians, officials and others under pressure, this book will show you how to stand up to what have been described as "blowtorch-on-the-belly" questions.

This is a technical term from the world of Australian politics – reputedly the place where dialogue is the most vicious in the democratic world.

It applies to situations where interrogators subject you to sustained, rugged, painful questioning – the kind you could expect in the most ferocious of media interviews for instance.

"Blowtorch-on-the-belly" questioning can also be deployed against you in the boardroom, in a career appraisal and anytime something's gone wrong and the finger of blame is pointing at you.

Doing badly when subjected to this kind of questioning can damage your career and even lose you your job.

Doing well through decisive, positive and uplifting answers can help propel you towards outcomes you want in the workplace and beyond.

As a media interviewer, I've watched some business leaders, officials and politicians set fire to their careers and public image by losing their tempers, their nerve and their dignity when put under pressure by myself and others.

I've also seen some of them do what the front cover of this book suggests and successfully put the fire out – sometimes seemingly with very little effort – and then inject powerful, positive ideas and visions into the conversation to move things in the direction they want.

One particularly memorable incident was when Britain's highly controversial Margaret Thatcher came to Sydney in the earlier years of her prime ministership. At the time she was administering harsh and unpopular cost-cutting medicine to the struggling economy of the UK. Our star tough-guy interviewer at the Australian Broadcasting Corporation couldn't land a glove on her as she gave him and our audience a stern lecture about the importance of the principle she called "sound money".

There was much to throw at her about the initial negative side-effects of the medicine – and the tough-guy interviewer didn't hold back from this. Yet the aptly named Iron Lady steamed through the interview as if a battle ship were being harried by the smallest of mosquitos.

I noticed the same phenomenon – of some politicians, business leaders and officials doing remarkably well in challenging interviews and some doing remarkably badly – when I became a foreign correspondent.

Shortly before the fall of the Iron Curtain in Europe, I got to subject the Polish Vice-Minister for Nuclear Energy in Warsaw to blowtorch-style questions about the dangers of communist-designed Chernobyl-era nuclear power stations in his country and the risk of another nuclear catastrophe in what was then the Soviet-dominated "Eastern Bloc". These questions resulted in a string of nervous, bumbling answers that were put to air on the BBC World Service, making him and his reactors appear dangerously inept.

In contrast, amidst the anti-communist "Velvet Revolution" in 1989 in Prague, I and other foreign correspondents got to ask the leading revolutionary Václav Havel about whether he would seek the presidency of what was then Czechoslovakia. We were swept away by the smoothness and power of his impressively thoughtful and eloquent – though sometimes artfully non-committal – answers, which raised his standing and made it all the more likely that he would become president. He swiftly did.

When planning this book I have looked back analytically over all the interviews that I've been privileged to do around the world. It became clear that there was a massive difference between the way various people reacted to "blowtorch-on-the-belly" questioning.

Some would metaphorically collapse in a quivering heap under blowtorch-style questioning.

Others would sail through the interrogation as they might steer a yacht in a gentle breeze.

Eventually I discovered what made the difference.

It was largely down to planning, preparation and practice.

With the benefit of hindsight it was clear that some politicians, business leaders and officials had been successfully trained to deal with tough interview questions and had worked at perfecting their replies and their delivery style in advance.

Those who shone out in rigorous interviews had typically done some training or had effectively trained themselves.

It eventually became public knowledge that Margaret Thatcher had had intense coaching – on the recommendation of the Hamlet-playing acting maestro Lord Laurence Olivier no less. This was most evident in the way Mrs Thatcher lowered her voice to sound more authoritative as her career progressed. In fact, one coaching session was – embarrassingly – recorded, leaked and publicly broadcast in Australia, Britain and elsewhere. But it showed what a dedicated communications student she became.

As a playwright and one-time stage hand, Václav Havel was surrounded by actors and clearly appreciated the value of rehearsing for those big moments in the spotlight. No wonder he was so impressive when I and my fellow foreign correspondents sought to test him out while he was holding a press conference on the stage at one of the Czechoslovakian theatres that became a focal point during his theatrically choreographed revolution.

The more I looked at it, the more I discovered that the art and science behind giving great answers is a learnable skill – and that those who shone out worked in advance on their content, their structure and their delivery style.

There are ways of combatting the hottest of blowtorch-on-the-belly questions and turning them to your advantage. The methods for successfully dealing with challenging questions from media interviewers can also be adapted to the tough questions you can get in the workplace from all kinds of sources – prospects, clients, colleagues, shareholders and financiers.

And if world leaders can train to improve their answers, then so can everyone else in the workforce.

When I started working as a lecturer in broadcast journalism in British colleges and universities on my pathway to being an international professional speaker, I was invited into the fascinating world of media and communications training.

Public Relations (PR) firms and training companies would ask me to come in and rough up their clients in mock blowtorch-on-the-belly media interviews and other challenging professional conversations to see how they coped – and then work with me to help their clients perform more confidently at a higher level.

I got to witness how the PR experts equipped their clients to answer emotionally-charged questions, horrible questions and tricky questions. And I could utilise my own particular area of expertise coming from Down Under – really ignorant questions … the kind that can cause some people to explode with rage.

I began teaching and developing the methods and golden formulae myself in one-to-one coaching sessions, master classes and conference speeches – sometimes even to audiences of PR people themselves.

The techniques work with apprentices seeking to change jobs, sports professionals being interviewed ahead of their next match, and sales teams and business leaders wanting to grow their empires across a vast range of industries.

And I found the techniques highly useful when facing questioning myself, as I increasingly did in my role as an international broadcasting commentator and newspaper critic.

Having been interviewed hundreds of times as a newspaper reviewer and commentator on Sky TV, the BBC and Al Jazeera, I have found the techniques to be especially useful when I have been asked questions on subjects where the information I had was limited or non-existent. They were particularly helpful, for example, when the newspapers for reviewing arrived late in the studio and I would be asked to comment on an article that I hadn't had the chance to look at. At this point I would need to utilize the golden formulae in order to (hopefully) gracefully manoeuvre the conversation onto an article that I had actually had the chance to read.

These methods proved particularly useful during the years I appeared weekly on BBC Radio 5 Live's Nicky Campbell Show with fellow London-based foreign correspondents from Russia and America. Our role was to answer questions about what we were reporting on and to explain what was happening in our own countries to the British audience. The golden formulae helped with responding to the unpredictable queries we would sometimes field from callers to the programme – and also with questions from Nicky himself, who is a master at blowtorch-wielding and putting interviewees on the spot.

But blowtorch-style questions aren't the only ones that put interviewees under pressure. People can also fall apart when asked softer questions too, and this book will help with that as well.

When I was recruiting potential students for university places in London, some highly intelligent candidates would self-destruct on the most simple and obvious question: "Why do you want to do this course?"

And as when the law-bending US President Richard Nixon was famously being interviewed by Britain's charming David Frost – often more a gentle tickler than a blowtorcher – it was sometimes the less forceful questions that brought the most damaging, self-incriminating responses. For example, it was a relatively under-stated question that prompted Nixon to give his infamous answer: "When the president does it, that means it's not illegal."

Tough questions are tough if they're tough for you. They can come to you in all sorts of forms.

Whether they lead you to drop the ball – or whether you hit them out of the park like a great cricketer or baseball player – is ultimately up to you.

What I hope you will find gratifying about using the techniques set out in this book is that they are based entirely on telling exact truths and nothing but truths.

Yes really!

It is true that some (not all) politicians abuse the formulae and misuse them in order to seek to avoid answering questions. But this is easily spotted by observant and discerning members of the viewing public (that probably includes you!).

Of course no one wants to resemble a question-evading politician when taking part in important conversations in the workplace, so this book will show you how to come across in a far more positive and helpful way.

When you know how to apply the techniques properly, you will be in a position to use truth as a highly effective weapon.

It will enhance your effectiveness, your confidence and your image.

The techniques will help you come up with the best possible answers to the worst possible questions.

If you know your stuff, you have a credible case and you can develop your ability to convey it, then the golden formulae will help you face up to challenging questions in all kinds of workplace situations – in meetings, job interviews, career appraisals, presentations, pitches to potential clients, price negotiations, as well as any form of public grilling.

This book will also help you know what to say when you don't know the answers, or when there is very little you can realistically say in particular circumstances – something I'm constantly asked about when helping those working in the world's growing number of call centres.

Part One contains easy-to-understand techniques and the golden formulae to help you with tactics, strategy and developing a winning approach to the tough questions you face now and will face in the future at work.

Part Two then shows how the learning can be applied to deal with the range of challenges and situations that commonly arise in various aspects of your working life, and where you need to be properly prepared and focused.

There are anecdotes and examples throughout, so you can picture in your mind how the techniques have succeeded and how you can make them work for you.

I've been blessed to have the opportunity to teach communications skills on six continents (Antarctica is still to come!). While minor adjustments to the approach may be needed in some parts of the world, I've developed and tested the techniques covered here across political and cultural boundaries – and for people at all levels in the workplace.

Giving great answers to tough questions at work is a learnable skill – for everybody everywhere.

The success of the methods explains why business leaders invite me to work with their people across hierarchies – from top teams, to sales and marketing teams, to technical operators and groups of emerging young stars.

The techniques enable those with an excellent case to get off the back foot onto the front foot. And they help those who have a less-than-excellent case to make the best of it – and to take action to enhance their case as well.

When you put the guidance from this book into practice, you will find yourself thinking less about the clever answers you should have given as you descend the stairs after losing verbal encounters, and starting to work out in advance the great winning answers to the tough questions you can often readily predict.

By boosting your answers, this book will make your life in the workplace more enjoyable, more effective and more successful. It will help enhance and protect your reputation.

It will be useful for anyone with ambition, who wants to be better equipped to make a difference at work and through their work.

And it will help you move closer to becoming what today's world of work needs more of – a game-changing inspirational communicator!

PART ONE

THE TOOLS YOU NEED

Here you'll find the tools you need in general terms in order to formulate and deliver great answers to those tough questions that can be fired at you at various times during your working life.

Part One introduces you to the play-to-win approach, which underpins the thinking throughout this book. Play-to-win here means, wherever possible, winning for you AND for the person asking you the tough questions – as well as for any additional audience in or outside the room.

This approach enables you to achieve a win/win or a win/win/win outcome, where you give answers that help you achieve your aims. At the same time, you'll provide your conversation partners and wider audience with the most useful, reassuring and inspiring things they need to know.

This part will equip you with, among other things, the two golden formulae for giving great answers to tough questions. These and other revelations can transform the way you view and take part in professional conversations now and in the future.

This is what routinely happens to participants who learn about the golden formulae in my communications-boosting master classes. When you understand the formulae, you tend to view verbal inter-actions involving you and those around you – and exchanges between others – in a different way.

You can see how those who are practiced in using the formulae – and those who have an instinct to act in line with them – come out better than others do time after time when they are verbally under scrutiny or under fire.

Knowing the formulae will help you become a better analyser of the conversational ecosystem around you. Putting the formulae into action in the workplace will propel you towards being a more successful player within it.

By the end of Part One you'll be set for what follows, where you'll be able to put these tools into action in a wide range of specific workplace situations both tomorrow and throughout your career.

So let's kick off now – and enjoy the first half of this two-part game that will empower you to operate more effectively, more wisely and more profitably in the vital world of workplace conversations by helping you and others achieve the outcomes you desire.

Chapter 1

WINNING ANSWERS EVERY TIME

Imagine you suddenly find yourself in charge of a bunch of four-year-olds about to play their first game of football.

The youngsters are revved up, have short attention spans and are under pressure to perform from their pushy parents. Amidst the excitement they could easily lose sight of what they're really meant to do.

Reduced to its simplest, your initial pre-match job as manager is to get across one clear over-riding message to the team members: "If you're going to win the game you have to score at least one goal – and more if you can."

Sure they'll need to keep the ball out of their own goalmouth. But even if they defend perfectly, they won't actually win the game unless they get the ball into their opponent's net at least once, and ideally more.

This may seem obvious. But in a broadly similar situation, when it comes to answering tough questions in the workplace, many people don't score any goals – and don't even try to.

Their approach is to go into that job interview, phone call with a hesitant prospect or potentially angry shareholder meeting and just hope that somehow they will scrape through to get an acceptable outcome without totally shredding their reputation.

Scoring a goal with every answer

A typical comment they make beforehand is: "I hope they ask me the right questions."

Or, more negatively, their plea is: "I hope they don't ask me THAT."

Alas, when it comes to situations such as these, the interview panel members, your prospect or the shareholders will often see it as their job to ask you the WRONG questions. They will often fire questions that are designed to score a goal against you. If you just defend without actually kicking any goals you will come out a loser, as will the four-year-old footballers.

Worse still, if you don't seek to kick goals then you're letting down the very people you ought to be convincing about your case – as well as yourself.

To come out as a winner you need to have the right winning mindset before the challenging conversation starts. This will help guide you towards the winning outcomes for you and others in the conversation.

Fundamental to this winning mindset is to realize that when you're being asked tough questions, there are always positive and helpful things you can say that will benefit the others involved.

However dire a situation is – even, tragically, if it involves injuries or deaths that could be seen as your organization's fault – in a tough professional conversation there are still goals you can and need to score and objectives you can achieve for the benefit of all those touched by what's happened.

And surprisingly to some, part of the art of scoring those goals includes actually answering those tough questions.

At the very least, your responses should involve explaining why you can't answer a particular question and then adding something extra that's useful and to the point. It always requires telling exact truths and nothing other than the truth. But it necessitates telling these exact truths in the best possible way. And it involves getting across a message – effectively scoring that goal – at every opportunity.

This means you should be seeking to score a goal every time a question comes to you.

I've found there are proven strategies involving highly effective techniques for giving great answers to all tough workplace questions. You will learn these secrets as the book progresses, but first we need to ensure the right mental approach – a win/win outlook – or when there is an audience beyond your questioner, a win/win/win outlook.

Let's go back to the football. Just suppose you did so well in getting the right message across to those four-year-olds that they won their first game as a result – and many more besides.

Eventually you come to be regarded as a football managing genius. You go on to manage older teams in bigger leagues. Ultimately you get put in charge of trying to win the next football World Cup – for the country of your choice.

Given the significance of the mission, there's one thing you certainly would not do. You wouldn't just turn up on the pitch with your players on the day of the first World Cup match and merely hope for the best.

You would pick your squad with great care and plan, prepare and practice for victory.

This may sound like a no-brainer. But when going into situations where they're facing tough questions, it's amazing how many otherwise intelligent people just "wing it".

Fascinatingly, this is not what most of the same people would do with their household spending, and not what business leaders would do with their company finances.

What you should do is implement the "3 Ps" of the verbal communications world – Plan, Prepare and Practice.

Instead, what too many people rely on is what pops into their head at the moment a tough – and often predictable – question is asked.

When explaining their lack of preparation, they sometimes reveal that they believe it's all about "thinking fast on your feet".

Now while being able to think quickly under pressure is a useful trait, in vital situations involving potentially career-killing questions you don't want to leave things to the whim of the moment. It's pretty hard for the most skilled of us to do this well with absolute consistency.

But it is possible for everyone in the workplace to consider in advance the questions they might face – and plan, prepare and practice in order to achieve the best possible result.

This plan, prepare and practice approach is effective for questions in everyday situations, which determine whether you end up having a good or a bad day at work. And it's effective in high-level cases at big moments that shape your long-term career prospects and potentially the outlook for your whole organization.

Taking inspiration from a master

Let's look at an instructive situation involving the head of Virgin, Sir Richard Branson.

In 2007 he suddenly faced questions over a fatal crash involving one of his company's trains in the Lake District of northern England.

The tragedy caused the death of an elderly woman, while the driver and dozens of passengers were injured. This is an awful situation for anyone to be interviewed about – all the more so when the reporters are asking you questions at the scene with the mangled wreckage of your company's colourfully branded train in the background.

Nonetheless, Sir Richard wisely cut short a family holiday in Italy to return to Britain to be questioned by the media swarm that had gathered at the scene of the crash.

He rightly declared it a very sad day – but he also made a series of positive points as well, all of which were hugely advantageous to Virgin, but also helpful to others.

Sir Richard hailed the company driver as "a hero" for the way he handled the situation when the train got into trouble.

He proclaimed the Virgin train to be "magnificent". It was "built like a tank", he declared, before adding: "If it had been any of the old trains the injuries and the mortalities would have been horrendous."

Sir Richard cleverly used one of his answers to put the crash in a vastly broader context, in order to highlight Virgin's historically good safety record. "I've been in the transportation business for nearly twenty-five years", he said, "and we've transported nearly half-a-billion people. Fortunately we've never had to be in this situation before".

Sir Richard had thoughts of condolence for the bereaved and of comfort for the injured. There was a Branson accolade for those who had the onerous task of helping the injured – the emergency services and Royal Air Force personnel – whom he praised for their "wonderful" response.

Finally, in a masterly worded answer that subtly shifted the focus away from Virgin, Sir Richard addressed the really tough question of who was responsible for the crash: "If it is the fault of the line then we've got to make sure it never happens again."

Taking proper care of the tracks was not Virgin's responsibility, so this answer seemed to hint that the responsibility might lay with the body in charge of track maintenance. This was something a court vindicated five years later, when Network Rail was fined £4 million after admitting health and safety breaches.

Off the back of a disaster, Sir Richard came across in a humane, concerned and dignified way while making Virgin look as good as it possibly could in adverse circumstances. Clearly he and his team planned and prepared before he stepped in front of the cameras. And his performance was so impressive that he had clearly benefited from previous practice in training (not with me) to face questions in tough media situations.

Admittedly Sir Richard sounded a touch hesitant at times. But that seemed right for the graveness of the situation. In fact, sounding too slick would have backfired terribly.

The result in terms of media coverage and brand protection was far better for Virgin than anyone could reasonably have expected. Sir Richard succeeded in turning the crisis of tough media questioning into an opportunity to convey positive messages of comfort, praise, reassurance and inspiration to those affected in various ways by the dreadful circumstances.

Sir Richard kicks goals and creates win/win/win when it counts – for his questioners, for himself and for his wider audience.

So can you.

Learning what *not* to do

Let's have a look at what can happen when someone does the opposite of what the Virgin leader did – without planning, preparation or practice and without inspiration.

This is a situation that I have had played out in front of me in master classes all too often. I ask for participants to write the worst question they could be asked and then demonstrate how they characteristically respond. In these days of ongoing pressure to reduce headcounts, it is often a question from employees to a boss like: "Are our jobs at risk?"

A typical and quite chilling answer from the boss is: "Yes, your jobs are at risk." Full stop. End of conversation!

Now you could say this answer is to be admired for its honesty and brevity. But there's not much else that's good about it.

An answer like this will have a demoralizing effect on the listener. It will have the same effect on their co-workers when they pass it on to others, as they surely will.

And bad news travels fast – even faster than the speed of light – as that embodiment of wisdom *The Hitchhiker's Guide to the Galaxy* observed. In fact, bad news travels faster still since the invention of the mobile phone and social media.

The boss's answer does nothing helpful for the workers or the company. It will probably result in a dramatic downturn in morale and productivity.

Workers will be more inclined to throw their energy into finding alternative employment rather than doing their best in a company that they think is about to get rid of them. And if the answer finds its way into the local media, as a result of a tip-off or a tweet, then the company will be in deeper trouble still.

So what should the boss have said?

Depending on the details of the situation, there are any number of things he could have stated that would still have been accurate, but far more inspiring.

We can't entirely quibble with his first word, "Yes". If the jobs are at risk then saying this is the right thing to do. However, it would be more empathetic and positive, while still honest, to say: "Regrettably, they're not as safe as we'd like them to be."

His next words – "your jobs are at risk" – constitute an own goal. What the boss is doing is repeating back a negative proposition. As he's already answered the question directly, he doesn't need to do this. Reinforcing the negative by regurgitating the downbeat language put to him is unnecessary and counterproductive.

Yet people do this all too frequently. Listen for it. What inspirational communicators do is choose their own words rather than repeat back the negatives of those questioning them. The key is to say what you want to say in your own words – and choose positive words wherever possible. Words have power, so keeping control of the vocabulary you deploy in the workplace is vital.

What then can the boss say to follow his initial negative admission?

Here's an uplifting option:

> "But we're doing everything possible to make your jobs as safe as they can be. The management team has put together a plan which involves…"

Or alternatively:

> "However we will do whatever we can to keep the entire team employed if at all possible. We plan to hold a meeting of all staff to look at everyone's suggestions for boosting productivity, cutting waste and increasing sales to put us in a stronger position…"

But let's suppose, despite all the noble efforts, that some of the jobs still have to go. This is not something the business leader should announce casually on the run when confronted in the workplace. At the same time, he shouldn't say anything other than an exact truth.

Whatever the situation, there will be positives he can point to that will be far better than what was originally said.

So his answer could include something like: "In the current economic downturn we will, very sadly, have to lose a few positions – but this will help protect the company and the rest of the workforce. We have had to do this in the past and it helped the firm to survive and then to later revive to become stronger than ever. In fact, some of the people working here today such as Mary and George had to go in the last recession. But we were able to ask them to rejoin as soon as things improved. Based on projected sales to newly emerging markets, we're expecting that if everyone puts in a big effort, in two years' time we'll be in a much better position than we are now – and that the overall size of our workforce will actually be larger."

What is happening in the suggested answers is that the boss is being a positive leader and is taking the initiative to go beyond the confines of the question.

He's also taking into account the effect that his answer will have on the asker – and the rest of his workforce.

These are vital aspects of being an inspirational communicator. Answering a question directly doesn't mean you have to be a slave to it. Under the rules of normal conversation you are allowed to say more. And in most cases you should.

This is frequently the case in the tough-question environment that people find themselves in at the start of their working life – and beyond: in the job interview.

A typically challenging job interview question is something like: "Why should we give you this job when some other applicants are better qualified?"

What happens all too often is that candidates say something unhelpful, such as "I don't know" or something against themselves like "Perhaps it was a mistake for me to have applied."

Yet there may be any number of ways in which the job seeker could capitalize on this question. It's worth remembering that a question like this is often just designed to test you out rather than to prosecute a serious case against you.

If you empower yourself to have a winning mentality, there is always a positive point you can make off the back of such a question.

Let's suppose the job is to be part of a team designing new electronic games.

It could be that the job seeker has had considerable experience at playing and inventing such games, which may be more compelling than actual qualifications.

So the start of the answer could be something like: "I have actually had considerable hands-on experience in this area, which other employers have found to be far more valuable than academic studies. I've been an enthusiastic player of these games since I was four years old and I've designed several of them myself that my friends love. Rather than going to university to study computer science, I went straight into the workforce because I couldn't wait to get involved in making the kind of games that I knew the younger generation are crying out for. For example…"

You can see that what you go on to say after dealing with the initial negative at the start of your answer is bound to be better if thought out in advance, rather than made up on the run.

And so often those negative questions are predictable.

If we return to the sporting world, people on the receiving end of a tough question typically end up playing beginner's ping-pong. The ball comes to them and they lob it back meekly to the inquirer in a way that makes the next shot against them all too easy. They reply within the narrow confines of the question, but do nothing extra. As a result, they become a prisoner of the question – especially if they repeat back any negatives that are part of the inquiry. This also sets them up for a follow-on question about the same topic that is often harsher than the first one.

The inspirational communicator breaks out of this potential cycle before it can start.

The trick is not to play ping-pong.

You need to play rugby – or American football.

Having answered the question, you need to pick up the ball, run down the field and put the ball down where you want it – scoring a try or a touchdown underneath the goalposts. This puts you in charge.

And remember, the tough questions often come to you when you are seen as the person knowing the most about the topic or the person in command. People can ask you the pertinent questions because it's expected that you are the one with the right knowledge. So how you answer is vital. And in giving your answer you are generally better off saying a bit more than just replying exactly to what is asked.

You are in the position of the giver. You can be generous. You should give of your time, expertise and effort. And in this way you also shift the focus to where you want it – the place where your interests and those of your questioner and any wider audience overlap.

In this manner you can escape from the lose/lose/lose model.

In professional conversations, if you don't score with your answers, then the questioner and the audience beyond may lose out as well. This sets up a demoralizing downward spiral where nobody wins.

So the aim is to strive for that win/win/win model. In this situation, if you score – and you should be seeking to score on every question – everybody comes out in front.

Winning answers in the right spirit

If we return to rugby, the inspirational answers game should be played in the spirit of the famous Barbarians Club. This club was founded on the principle of always playing exciting, clean, attacking rugby to the highest standards. Excellent sportsmanship is expected from the "BaaBaas" and their opponents. While both sides play to win, matches involving the Barbarians seek to have the game played foremost for the enjoyment and glory of the sport.

A top Barbarian's game will involve great style, great tries and a great spirit. Who gets the higher score still matters, but it is less important than that a splendid game is had. So, played in the right spirit both sides and the spectators in the stands – as well as those watching on television – all come away uplifted.

It should be the same highest aspiration underpinning truly great answers to tough questions in the working world. All involved end up in a better position as a result of the tough questions being asked and answered impressively. Everybody gains.

Giving inspirationally positive, rather than demoralizingly negative, answers has always been a plus in the workplace. In today's world of instant communications, getting it right is more important than ever before. Taking into account the presence of YouTube, Twitter, Facebook, 24-hour rolling news and mobile phones and their in-built cameras, what you do, what you say and how you say it matter more – because organizations and the people working in them are potentially more visible now than ever before.

You don't have to be a prince in Britain's royal family to know that the old saying "What happens in Las Vegas stays in Las Vegas" no longer applies. Whether it's photos of you playing strip billiards with people you've just met in a Las Vegas bar, or giving badly worded answers to your professional colleagues or entering into a discussion on social media without giving your comments proper thought, what you do and say can be transmitted instantly. And it's potentially out there in cyberspace forever.

Observing how _not_ to do it

For better or worse, the world of communications has changed.

Perhaps the most profound high-profile case of someone not appearing to understand this involved the one-time Chief Executive of BP, Tony Hayward, during the Gulf of Mexico oil spill disaster in 2010. This was the largest accidental marine oil spill in the history of the petroleum industry, resulting from an explosion at the Deepwater Horizon well. The disaster killed eleven men working on the platform and injured seventeen others. There was an outflow of millions of barrels of crude oil that devastated wildlife and crippled the local fishing industry.

In answering questions about the crisis, Tony Hayward committed what, in my view, was gaffe after gaffe with a speed and routine efficiency that was hard to keep up with.

Now admittedly, standing up to massive emotional and media pressure in the global spotlight is a challenging thing to do. But if Mr Hayward had demonstrated that he fully grasped the communication rules for our age and some basic principles of normal human emotional response, I believe he would have avoided trashing his own and the company's reputation. He also may have helped prevent billions being wiped off BP's share price and he could possibly have even kept his job.

Instead, among his comments was one that has been and will be remembered for a very long time to come – when he declared to reporters in Florida, with breath-taking self-indulgence: "I would like my life back."

This comment came to symbolize what was perceived – perhaps unfairly – as a real lack of concern by BP for what had happened. Ironically it came as part of an answer where Mr Hayward was commendably, though somewhat belatedly, expressing an apology to those affected by the disaster. But he ended up being portrayed as feeling more sorry for himself than the families and friends of those killed in the tragedy, the oil-soaked pelicans and the instantly impoverished Gulf of Mexico fishing teams.

The adverse and emotionally charged responses to Mr Hayward's comment came from far and wide – and remain on the web for anyone to Google.

But you don't have to be a captain of industry to be caught up as the self-created victim of shocking answers.

Whether it's seeking your first job, getting your annual appraisal or being queried by a prospect, you and those you interact with benefit when you give great answers to their tough questions.

Whatever line of work you're in, or aspire to be in, this book will show you how to drastically reduce or eliminate verbal mistakes.

It will show you how to stand up to tough questions – one-to-one, in a group or with a mass audience.

It will show you how to get your content right, your structure right and your delivery right.

The really good news is that giving inspirational answers to tough questions is a learnable skill.

When there's a strong case behind what you're saying, you can become virtually bombproof.

So if you haven't already, please ponder: "What is the worst profes-sional question someone could ask me at work?"

Write it down in the following box.

By the end of the book, you will know what a great answer to it is and you will feel a whole lot better about responding to this question.

You may even find yourself actually looking forward to the time when someone asks it!

And when you develop this kind of positive mentality you can go an amazingly long way – and come out winning every time.

"What is the worst professional question someone could ask me at work?"

Write your answer here...

Chapter 2

CRAFTING THE RIGHT MESSAGE TO UNDERPIN EVERY ANSWER

I was walking through a clearing in an English wood when two hyperactive, fluffy young husky-like Samoyeds bounded into view.

I'm not particularly dog-orientated, but I couldn't help thinking these bouncy puppies were especially adorable and particularly "pattable".

However, contrary to first appearances, they weren't interested in getting attention from me.

They headed straight for me, but then shot right past and began whisking around in big circles sniffing furiously at the ground and seeming somewhat perturbed.

When the puffed-out owner caught up with them he explained: "They're confused – because they can't find your dog."

If I were to really connect with his Samoyeds I needed to have something they were interested in – a four-legged friend of my own that they could sniff and chase... or perhaps some dog biscuits.

When you are seeking to connect with an audience of two-legged creatures it's the same. You must ensure you have something they're interested in.

And while your audience members often don't know it, when they're asking you questions, what they typically need from you is A MESSAGE.

And not just any message.

They need a message that hits the "What's In It For Me?" factor, which is specifically targeted at them.

Your answers will be so much more powerful and appreciated if they focus on what your audience is really interested in – and, wherever possible, touch on an aspect of the topic asked about that really benefits them.

As with dogs, if you can provide something of value to humans, then humans are more likely to want to engage.

Crafting that message your questioners need

To really connect with your questioners you must captivate them.

This does not mean telling them exactly what they want to hear.

You clearly don't tell them something if it's not true, appropriate or possible to deliver – however much they might like to hear you say it.

But when answering tough questions you typically don't want to be giving just facts alone. People who give great answers do more than merely convey facts.

Great answers in the workplace don't resemble answers in a quiz, where it's a matter of coming up with one or a few of the right words that will head you towards winning the prize.

To give a great answer you need to get across a clear message, just as you would have had to do when managing those four-year-old footballers in the first chapter.

A message can contain facts – and that can be a good thing.

But a message is a bigger concept than one or more facts.

It is far more than that, as an effective message leaves the audience with something distinct to contemplate, react to and possibly act upon – and hopefully even to benefit from.

The message is the major underlying point that the audience ultimately takes away.

The multiple championship-winning golfer Gary Player had a message for people wanting to know how to become really good at a sport.

"The harder I practice the luckier I get", he declared, popularizing a saying that is credited to various golfers and non-golfers.

It's a clever line, whoever thought it up first. The reason it works and is so memorable is because it contains such a powerful underlying message.

Gary Player's message to would-be champions is incredibly simple: "To become really good at a sport you need to work at it."

That doesn't sound nearly as slick or inspiring as the quote itself, but it is the fundamental message behind the saying.

Determine your message first, then formulate your answer

You typically want to establish what your message is first, before working out the detail of a great answer.

So when you're planning your response to an expected tough question, at the outset you should determine what your message for the audience is on the subject of the question.

To help you work out what your message is, ask yourself this question: "What do I want the listener/s to be thinking or feeling or doing after our conversation?"

You may or may not end up including your message directly in your answer. But your message is what will guide the direction of it. Once you are clear on what the message is, then it's so much easier to work out how the answer should be phrased.

Sometimes there will be a place within your answer for the precise message, exactly as you have written it. Sometimes you won't need to say the message explicitly as part of the answer – though it should nonetheless come across to your audience.

But once you have become clear in your own mind about the message you want to convey to a particular audience, you will make it so much easier to find the actual words you need to use.

By starting with the outcome of the conversation you have in mind, you can determine the message or messages to drive things towards that outcome by the way you word your answers.

What is the message?

A businesswoman flies into a financial district of a city to present and answer questions about her company's latest product – a breakthrough new medicine.

She makes a brief presentation and answers questions from the gathering of potential investors. Then she gets back into her helicopter to visit another city.

Suppose someone were to arrive late at the venue just after she had left and wanted to know what had been said.

If the businesswoman had done a superb job, those in the audience would find it easy to pass on the essence of what she imparted.

They might say: "We can potentially make big money by investing in her revolutionary new medicine that purports to cure cancer and will therefore make the world a better place."

The businesswoman could rightfully be pleased with this. If that's what most people were thinking afterwards, and these thoughts were indeed in line with the substance of what she said, then she could consider that she'd successfully conveyed her message.

And if she had taken the trouble to write down her central message beforehand to guide her, then the actual message itself was probably something even more succinct.

The message would be something like: "Invest in our breakthrough cancer cure to make big money for yourself and a happier world for everyone."

If the businesswoman did a good job in persuading the audience, she would naturally have provided some proof points to back up her contention that the medicine cures cancer. She would also have given further proof points to underpin the soundness of the proposed investment opportunity. For the moment, let's assume she had such proof points and conveyed them well.

Her number one task with the audience is to convey her message about the opportunity and benefits of the breakthrough.

At the centre of every great answer is a great message that comes across clearly and credibly – and with some emotional punch.

It will typically be positive, but it doesn't have to be.

A strong negative message can sometimes be appropriate and effective. Your accountant might usefully warn you: "If you don't pay your taxes on time, you'll have to pay extra."

To underpin your great answers on your topic you need a message that is succinct, powerful and which will stick with your audience.

But before we go any further into what makes a great message, we need to go deeper.

We need to go into what is at the heart of you and/or your organization.

Here's why…

What's at the heart of you?[1]

Picture a giant tree – one of those so-called "emergents", which breaks through the rainforest canopy and towers above the jungle around it.

The leaves are bright green, healthy and attractive.

And it's the leaves we mostly see as we look down at the rainforest from a distant hill. They are what visitors to the forest typically focus on.

But there is a lot more to the tree than its leaves.

Holding the leaves in place are stems and twigs. Supporting the stems and twigs are the branches. Propping up the branches is the massive trunk.

Of course the whole structure would topple over if it weren't for one extra vital thing: the massive root system.

It's this root system that effectively underpins the tree and sucks up water and nutrients to anchor the tree in place and allow it to have stability and life.

In this analogy, the leaves are the words that make up our answers. This is what listeners hear.

But there needs to be considerable substance behind those words to ensure your answers are truly great.

---

[1] The rainforest analogy here is based on a concept developed by Jo Pearson – media trainer, corporate film producer and former news-reader and journalist with *Eyewitness News*, Melbourne.

The stems represent the thoughts behind the actual words of the answers.

The twigs are the bigger ideas that prompt the individual thoughts.

The branches are emblematic of the policies and propositions behind the individual thoughts and ideas.

The trunk represents the guiding philosophy that underpins those policies and practices. It embodies the central purpose of the tree.

And the root system – upon which the tree's whole existence depends – represents the core values.

For us, it's these core values and the central purpose that provide the reason we get out of bed in the morning to go to the places where we answer the questions and all the other things we do.

The core values and central purpose are fundamentally what we stand for – whether we can immediately identify them or not.
So that you can become sure of your own core values, here are some questions for you to contemplate now – or when you next have some thinking time.

• What do you stand for?
• What is at the heart of you?
• Why do you do what you do?
• What is the fundamental purpose of your work at the moment?

When you know the answers to these kinds of questions you have a fantastic root system to support you – to nourish and strengthen the policies and propositions that underpin the answers you ultimately give.

It's good for you to personally know the answers to these questions.

It may also be helpful for you to answer the same questions on behalf of your organization.

If you have a good organizational mission statement, the core purpose will be recognized within it.

If you have a poor, bureaucratic, wishy-washy mission statement, then think about getting it upgraded to plain, powerful English so it's something everyone can grasp – something you and your team can wholeheartedly believe in and explain to others. It will give you stronger foundations for answering questions.

More than 400 years before the birth of Jesus Christ, the wise Greek philosopher Socrates decreed: "Know thyself."

Socrates was famous for asking probing questions. If you know yourself, you are better placed to answer such questions.

When you know the purpose of yourself and your organization, you have a strong root system to support everything we see above the ground – and you have much with which to inspire your messages that lie behind those great leafy answers.

For me and my organization, our central purpose is to help people around the world become inspirational communicators.

What is it for you?

Formulating your key message

When you know yourself and what you stand for, it becomes easier to help others – in relation to answering their questions and in other ways.

So when planning for a situation involving questions from an audience, you want to find out what you can about them.

Whether that audience consists of one questioner face-to-face; hundreds at a conference; thousands taking part in a radio phone-in; or potentially tens of thousands in an internet hook-up, you need to get inside their heads.

Fundamental to being able to give great answers is to have a good understanding of those asking you the questions and those listening to your answers.

In a big audience, not all members will be thinking the same way on every issue of course. If possible, you will want to be aware of various groups represented within any audience so you have a better idea of the different interests lurking behind them.

But there may well be some common thoughts and feelings amongst all audience members.

The key word here is "empathy". It's the capacity to place yourself in the shoes of others.

When you can do that, it's so much easier to formulate great answers to satisfy and inspire those audiences.

So if you're doing a presentation that will involve a question and answer session, you want to find out from the event organizer what you can about the audience:

- How much do they know about the topic you will be talking about?

- What might their existing views on it be?

- What is it that they will be most wanting to know on the topic?

Your audience members will typically have an agenda in any situation. This is what they want to get out of the session and what they would like to get out of you. You can often work out what that agenda is.

And of course, in any situation you will typically have an agenda too – based on your core values, central purpose and other parts of your tree.

These two agendas will not necessarily be the same, but they will overlap at some points, as represented in this diagram.

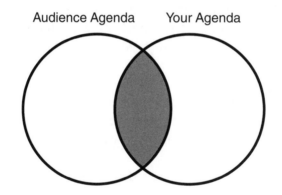

When you do your planning for an important encounter, you should aim for the overlap point in this diagram.

This is where there is a win/win between you and your audience.

So this is where your messages should be focused.

Let's make it real with a common situation where questions and answers are critical to the outcome for both sides: that is, a job interview.

Imagine you are an applicant seeking your dream job on the sales team at Latest Generation Funfair Games Corporation. The company produces modern and innovative versions of the kind of coin-operated machines people play on at fun piers, theme parks and amusement arcades.

You have a special interest in the company because since childhood you have been a fan – some might say an addict – of the kinds of machines the corporation produces. This was as a result of you being brought up in a seaside town with a fun pier where such machines proliferate. Since gaining your business degree you have developed a successful record in sales in a variety of products and also in managing various aspects of companies while maintaining a strong personal interest in the coin-operated machines through your children, who share your enthusiasm for them.

You would naturally do a bit of research on the funfair corporation and interrogate any contact you had beforehand to find out what they think the interview panel *really* wants.

Let's assume you discover that the number one thing they're looking for is someone who is exceptionally persuasive in difficult selling conditions because sales have been down lately. A couple of their recent machines have been commercial flops and the corporation is wondering what it can do to tap more effectively into the minds of modern-day youngsters to find out what they really want from their kind of machines – given strong competition from computer games.

You can probably give a whole bunch of reasons why you are a great person to have in any workplace. You might be very good at controlling budgets, organizing holiday rosters and putting on fantastic Christmas parties.

But useful though these qualities are, the interview panel is going to be fixated on getting someone who can help boost sales fast by persuading potential customers to buy and existing customers to buy more. And they would also be open to anyone who can help them design machines that the current marketplace is hungry for.

You can hit the right spots for the corporation, but the full range of your other qualities probably won't be high on the panel's agenda.

So, as you plan your application and interview performance, you look over your work history and evaluate your skillset with a view to focusing primarily on your ability as a persuader and seller and, capitalizing on your experience in using the machines they produce. You also seek to position yourself as someone well placed to advise the designers on what will have most appeal to buyers and their consumers.

Be aware that while you are determining how best to appeal to the corporation, it also works the other way around. The panel will be focusing on how to grab the services of the person they most want.

Assuming you come across as the standout hotshot salesperson with the right understanding of their product and marketplace, they need to make sure you end up with them and not a rival company, which may also be struggling with sales.

Let's also suppose you have recently inherited a large sum of money, so your main motivation to get the job is because you love the idea of working in the games area of your childhood, not because of the salary size. But you do like travelling around while you work, so the prospect of visiting different parts of the world on sales missions appeals to you.

The panel may have won clearance to pay 15% above the standard market rate in order to attract the right person.

However, this is not of great interest to you. Offering a big financial incentive to get the right person is on their agenda but it isn't on yours.

So if the panel members decide you are perfect for the job, and you simultaneously receive another job offer, they would need to come up with something other than a big salary to win your services. Giving you a key role in sales missions overseas might be a way of getting you on board.

So you need to work out how to appeal to their agenda and, if they want you, they will have to work out how to appeal to your agenda.

There are some obvious questions they will want to ask you, and some obvious ones you will want to ask them.

From your perspective, you will want to focus your answers on how persuasive you are as a seller, how good you are at helping others to sell and your intimate knowledge of what attracts young people to play particular machines.

And in order to test how persuasive you are, the panel will have an incentive to put you under big pressure to see if you have what it takes to handle what sales folk call "objections" to buying.

So when it comes to preparing for the interview, you will need to focus on their primary need and come across as being as persuasive as possible.

You naturally won't know exactly the questions they will ask – but it is pretty easy to work out the kind of questions they might be.

Whatever the final form of those questions, you want to get across one central positive message, such as:

"I am a highly persuasive salesperson who is well placed to help you sell a lot more because of my experience, studies and longstanding personal experience with your types of products."

You will also want to develop some additional related messages, which could be:

- "I have a strong track record in selling in difficult times."

- "I am effective at showing others how to improve their selling skills so I can help other team members."

- "Because of my longstanding interest since I was six years old in playing the kinds of games you make, I will be able to help advise on product development to better appeal to the market."

Of course you will need to have proof points and examples at your fingertips to back up these points so that they will believe you.

And you know that you must be focused in the interview on getting these messages across if you are to be offered the job.

So whatever questions they ask you, these messages should come across in different ways in virtually every answer to every question.

Crafting that great message

So what makes a great message?

It boils down to something short and simple – but there should be much substance behind it.

When facing up to a particular challenging situation, you typically want one headline message.

This is where, if an objective report were to be written on the conversation, your message would be in the headline of the story.

This is the big message that guides all that you say. It can be one of those messages that you actually say directly, as part of one or more of your answers.

You will need to get that message in your head and make sure everything you say is consistent with it.

So, in the case of the job interview situation at the funfair corporation, the headline message could be: "I can help you take sales of your machines to new heights because of my wide-ranging sales experience and understanding of the young consumers who are the ultimate buyers of your products."

But you can also have other additional messages as well – providing they are consistent with the headline message.

You can regard these as supplementary messages or, if they are on exactly the same topic, as sub-messages.

You don't want to have too many supplementary or sub-messages overcrowding your brain.

Having about three is often good.

But always work out your overarching headline message first.

One huge advantage of having a great headline message is that it is something to fall back on if, at any point, you don't know quite what to say.

If you have a blank moment, or are asked a question you momentarily find impossible to deal with, you can at least come back to your headline message.

The great headline message underpinning your great answers should encompass a number of virtues.

It has to be true – and credible.

Great messages are typically expressed in a single sentence; though sometimes it is good to break them in two.

While being succinct – even terse – the message says a lot.

Great messages don't have to sound especially eloquent, though it's splendid if they do.

They could be the springboard for the creation of a snappy, catchy slogan in the advertising world or a short, sharp, punchy 15-second "soundbite" designed to grab attention and stick in the mind, but they don't have to be.

In your initial planning it's more important to get the message right for the particular audience and the particular situation, rather than for it to sound brilliant.

Here is a message that doesn't sound particularly slick or sexy, but is potentially effective when deployed in the right conversation:

> "Tests have shown that this new tablet results in faster, more effective relief for upset stomachs than any other pill previously invented."

Eloquent it is not. But it makes the point clearly and could provide excellent underpinning to a conversation in a medical environment with someone who is prone to stomach aches or someone responsible for buying tablets for a medical institution.

When you get to the point of phrasing specific answers to questions in this area, you may find a way of expressing the message with more pizzazz.

And it's excellent if you can.

But it works as an underlying message by being short, direct and easy to understand.

Combining fact and emotion in your message

A great message also contains an emotional element as well as a factual element.

Excellent communication involves a balance between facts and emotion.

If it's all factual, your content could be seen as too dry and dull.

If it's all emotional, your content could be seen as hysterical and out-of-control.

You can think of a great message as being like a train speeding along the tracks towards its destination.

The tracks guide the direction of the train's journey. They represent the factual underpinning of the message.

We can regard this as the GUIDANCE element.

But the train needs some kind of energy to allow it to move. This energy – diesel, electricity or steam – allows the train to progress. The energy represents the emotional content of the message.

We can regard this as the PUSH element.

The train won't get anywhere without both elements – tracks and energy.

Your message won't get anywhere without both elements – GUIDANCE and PUSH.

This allows you to satisfy both minds and hearts!

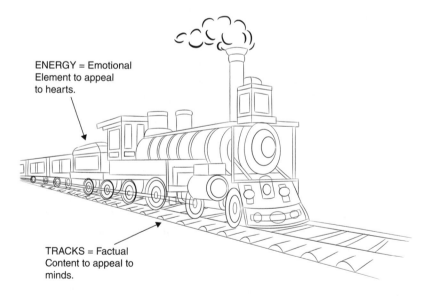

ENERGY = Emotional Element to appeal to hearts.

TRACKS = Factual Content to appeal to minds.

The factual element for the message involving the new tablet for stomach ache is contained within the part that says tests have shown it works faster and more effectively than any other pill previously invented.

But relief from a severe stomach ache is actually deeply emotional. Think of how bad it feels when a stomach ache is at its worst. And think of how good it feels when a stomach ache vanishes. So the message has this emotional element as well, which is focused on the emotive word "relief".

To reinforce the point about the need for both the guidance and the push elements, let's take another situation.

It concerns a new fictional offering we can call Product X.

The product is designed to be dissolved in water – which is, as a chemist will tell you, two parts hydrogen and one part oxygen. So here is some factual content.

But let's suppose the amazing thing about Product X, which is incorporated in the message you need to craft to sell it, is that when you put it in water, and then splash it behind your ears, it makes you desirable to anyone you want to desire you. So this is the emotional content.

Would you like some?

The last element in the message provides a powerful emotional punch. You can imagine that – when invented – the product will race off the shelves.

A great message with a strong emotional component also has the stickiness factor, so your audience will remember it long after it's been delivered.

When planning your answer for an expected tough question, think about the message you want to convey before you work out the exact words of your answer.

If you come up with a fantastically snappy, powerful and memorable way to word the message, that's marvellous.

In such cases you can include this wording within your great answer, which we will tackle in subsequent chapters.

Occasionally the message itself can actually work as a direct part of the answer.

Whether or not you actually say the exact message that you've worked out, it should always be the guiding light behind your answers.

Behind every great answer is a great message.

And as Gary Player might tell you, the more you practice crafting the right messages to underpin your answers, the luckier you'll get when it comes to receiving the right questions and achieving the right results after delivering your great answers.

Chapter 3

HARNESSING THE POWER OF STORIES

Having been brought up on the coast of Sydney, I've been happily spoilt when it comes to experiencing wonderful city beaches. Nonetheless, I was swept away when I got to speak at a conference in Rio de Janiero and had the chance to explore the coastline of this vibrant Brazilian city.

The beaches of Rio are magnificent.

Apart from great waves, soft sands and coconut palms along the fringes, they have spectacular views of the mountains and rocks that plunge dramatically into the Atlantic Ocean. The always-passionate Brazilians love them.

The biggest name is Copacabana. This beach is impressive, but it tends to get overwhelmingly busy. Because it's such a magnet, it bustles with locals seeking – quite understandably – to sell you all kinds of things at every opportunity.

The beach immediately next to it, Ipanema, is more idyllic. It's less overtly touristy and even more pleasant to bask on. There is just enough commercialism to keep you going. If you are thirsty, you can pay a coconut dealer to use a machete to vigorously slice through the husk and give you a straw to drink the refreshingly chilled milk inside.

Popularized by the 1960s song *The Girl From Ipanema*, the Brazilians adore Ipanema Beach. They flock to it – with lithe women in bikinis jumping around playing beach volleyball and bronzed men running along the beach getting even fitter and more tanned.

The hotel where I was speaking to British diplomats and their support teams fronted Ipanema Beach, and when I arrived before the conference began I felt the immediate urge to get out and mix with the Brazilians and foreign visitors on the sands and in the water.

In the uplifting South American sunshine, I ran all the way along Ipanema Beach. The sights, sounds and overall buzz were invigorating.

As I got towards the Copacabana end of the beach, you'll never guess what happened next?

Absolutely nothing.

But I bet you thought I was going to tell you a story!

The thing about stories is that people want them, like them and can't get enough of them.

As a result, stories have power.

You can tap into this power in parts of your great answers to tough questions.

Using stories to enhance your answers

Stories capture people's imaginations everywhere. Stories persuade. Stories can help you to do your job better and get a better job.

Stories have changed the world.

Stories will change the world still more.

Stories should be integrated into your challenging professional conversations.

Throughout history, great communicators have told stories.

Bigtime religious leaders told stories…

The Buddha told stories.

Mohammed told stories.

Moses told stories.

Jesus Christ told stories.

When people asked Jesus tricky questions about life, he told such memorable, captivating stories that they were even given a special name: parables.

There's the parable of the farmer sowing seeds in the field and the parable of the Good Samaritan. Jesus used parables to convey messages about how people should live. They are still read from the Bible's New Testament and retold again and again.

Jesus's stories – and the whole story of Jesus – are a key factor behind why he is still remembered a couple of thousand years on, whether or not you accept his religious viewpoint. His stories help explain why his statue has such a prominent position on the most prominent peak towering above the beaches of Rio.

Doing it like the presidents do

American presidents and other US leaders routinely capitalize on the power of stories.

Over the years, they have conveyed stories in all sorts of contexts – and not always about the past. Sometimes there is a strong element of story when they lay out their vision and ambitions for the future.

Near the start of the 1960s, President John F. Kennedy told what was effectively a story about how he believed America should, by the end of the decade, put a man on the moon and bring him safely back to earth. This helped persuade Congress to back the expensive space programme that enabled the story to turn into reality in July 1969 when the first moonwalks took place – six years after the president's terrible assassination.

Further into America's space programme, in 1986 when the space shuttle Challenger tragically exploded in the sky on its outward journey, President Ronald Reagan told his nation and the world what was effectively a story. He declared that the seven pioneers inside the spacecraft had slipped the surly bonds of earth to "touch the face of God". I was in North America at that time of national shock and grief, and witnessed how the devastated Americans loved their president for this story, which he used as part of what was known as his "mourner-in-chief" role.

Great stories prompt change

Stories touch people emotionally. They can comfort. They can persuade. They can inspire.

One of the most famous speeches ever – the "I Have A Dream" speech by American civil rights leader Martin Luther King – tells the story of King's dream that his four small children would one day live in a nation where they wouldn't be judged by the colour of their skin but by the content of their character.

Notwithstanding America's ongoing racial challenges, the dream has moved to a large extent towards becoming reality. Martin Luther King's story is still remembered and quoted in efforts to turn the story into total truth – long after his shocking murder.

Whether they are about the past, the present or the future, stories have a power that is not just for great speeches. They should be equally at home as a key part of your great answers to tough questions.

Let me explain why it's so important to utilize them.

In the last chapter we focused on the importance of having a powerful message at the heart of your great answers. But the thing about most messages is that they are typically based on assertion. Our job seeker, for example, was asserting that he was equipped to help the games company make more sales.

Important though such assertions are, the human brain logically requires proof points to back them up if they are to be believable.

Stories, which are often simply real-life examples, can be the proof points to support your message and ensure it comes across as being real and credible.

Painting pictures in the minds of your audience

When you are telling stories you are, on the face of it, sharing a carefully constructed series of words with your audience. But what is really happening if you are doing it well is that you're using those words to paint moving pictures in the minds of your listeners. If you're really good you will be using these words and pictures to direct the emotions in the hearts of your audience.

When you do it supremely well you get people coming out with responses like "I can see what you mean". What they are effectively saying, of course, is that they can visualize it in their imagination.

There is a variety of ways that you can provide effective proof points for your audience to back up your messages.

Stories and examples are amongst the most powerful and persuasive.

But the proof points can also consist of relevant facts and figures. They can be insightful observations. They can be metaphors or analogies. The earlier analogy of the tree in the forest to represent the core values, purpose and thoughts behind your answers is an example of an attempt to put a picture in your mind to back up a message.

Great communicators are aware of the need to deploy stories and examples to make their ideas real to people – and so that their audiences can easily grasp what they mean.

They especially need to use stories and examples if they are dealing with the abstract. This is because abstract concepts, important though they often are, need to be illustrated in our minds to enable audiences to picture what is meant.

Great communicators make a point of automatically backing up their more abstract thoughts with concrete examples.

Going up and down the abstract ladder

To underline the importance of this, let me draw upon a concept called the "Ladder of Abstraction", popularized by a most intriguing professor of the English language who went on to become an American senator. His name was Samuel Ichiye Hayakawa.

Hayakawa set out the "Ladder of Abstraction" concept in a brilliant book called *Language in Thought and Action*. I was blessed to have it issued to me as a textbook in my Sydney high school – just the thing to read on Manly or Long Reef Beach!

I admired the ladder concept then – and used it in school debating competitions to make sure that a good abstract point was always illustrated with a concrete example. When I began lecturing in journalism and running communications-boosting master classes I gravitated to the ladder, and have become something of a Hayakawa disciple.

The ladder of abstraction

Samuel Ichiye Hayakawa was a Canadian-born academic of Japanese ancestry who migrated to the United States and eventually went to Washington as a politician to represent the state of California.

His "Ladder of Abstraction" concept identifies the fact that there are different levels of language used that range from the general to the specific.

On the bottom rungs of the ladder are concrete things, which are easy to identify and see.

On the top rungs of the ladder are abstract concepts that are bigger, more ethereal and can be harder to envisage.

Highly effective communicators tend to metaphorically move up and down the ladder with considerable frequency. This helps to keep their audiences fully in the picture by allowing them to grasp both the general and the specific.

If someone gets stuck at the top of the ladder for too long they are in danger of talking as if viewing the world from that mythical ivory tower – making it hard for listeners to picture what they are thinking.

If someone gets stuck at the bottom of the ladder for too long they can bury their listeners in a heap of details, with the audience struggling to see how they fit together to make sense. They give too many fragments of the situation on the ground and we don't get the much-needed panoramic overview.

Great responses to questions often involve either going up or down the ladder in the story component of your answer.

Understanding Hayakawa's "Ladder of Abstraction" and utilizing it enables you to give better answers because your listeners are able to more readily grasp your overall point, but with sufficient detail to be able to visualize the pictures you are portraying.

Taking a journey down that ladder

Let's take a journey down the ladder so that you can grasp the concept fully with some pictures in your mind. We'll do so with the help of the Continent of Africa, where I have had the privilege of working with some heroic United Nations officials and dedicated local peacemakers.

Picture, at the top of the ladder, all the life in Africa.

Now you don't need to have trekked through Africa to realize that there is a lot of life sprawled across this vast continent. This is a big abstract concept, because there is so much life there – with different landscapes, different tribes, different migrant groups and so many different animals and plants.

So let's come half way down the ladder and picture just one African species. Imagine all the elephants in Africa. Can you see them wandering through the jungle, each elephant following the next in a giant grey line with their large wrinkled trunks trailing behind those skinny tails of the elephants in front? This is easier to picture because it's more specific than the overwhelming multitude of life at the top of the ladder.

Now let's come right down to the foot of the ladder and consider one single example of life in Africa.

He's a giraffe called Jock.

Jock lives at what is known as the Giraffe Centre on the outskirts of Nairobi in Kenya, East Africa. You may well ask why a Kenyan giraffe has a Scottish name. The answer, I suspect, has something to do with the fact that the Giraffe Centre was started by a man called Jock who was the Kenyan grandson of a Scottish Earl.

Whatever the origins of Jock the giraffe's name, there are three things you need to know about him. The first is that even by gargantuan giraffe standards, Jock is a really big boy. The second is that Jock is especially interested in food, as there is a mighty lot of Jock to feed. The third thing is that Jock is used to tourists being a good supply channel of food, and as a result he has an especially friendly approach towards humans.

Jock can roam for miles around the Giraffe Centre, but when I met him he was characteristically hanging about near the tourist entrance. This is because just near the entrance is a high wooden structure that forms the giraffe-viewing platform. You climb up and find, on the platform, a bucket that Jock is particularly interested in. Inside the bucket are little yellow fluffy balls called "giraffe food". You can put your hands in and scoop up the food. Then, if you hold out your hands, Jock will come over, lower his towering neck, and stick out his giant tongue that's bluey-grey and extremely slobbery. And you can have the experience that I did, of having Jock gobble up all the giraffe food from your hands and wait for you to go back to the bucket and get him some more.

Can you see Jock the giraffe? Can you hear him slurping up the giraffe food from your hands? Can you feel how yucky and sticky your hands get when they're covered in giraffe saliva? But can you feel how uplifting it is to be next to a creature who is soooo much bigger than you are and yet is so friendly and gentle?

So what have you just done? You have gone from the top of the "Ladder of Abstraction" with that crowded, hard-to-comprehend vision of all the life in Africa and climbed right down the bottom to contemplate one particular example of an African life that you can see, hear, feel and maybe even have feelings about.

So that's what needs to happen for your listeners when you give an answer that spells out a general concept. You should then take them down the ladder and present them with an example that is sufficiently vivid that they can see, hear and feel it – and possibly even care about it as well.

This is how you can harness the power of stories and examples and fluctuate up and down the "Ladder of Abstraction" within your great answers – and give your replies to questions all the more impact as a result.

Collecting illustrations for your treasure chest

When you need to engage in an exercise in persuasion and to answer challenging questions that are bound to arise along the way, you can hopefully see the value of having the right examples and stories lurking ready for deployment at the edge of your brain.

It's ideal to amass a whole treasure chest of these illustrations and to go over in advance how you will convey them, as you might do when planning to tell a joke.

You can keep the treasure chest physically in a box on your desk or in a file on your computer. Eventually you will need to ensure that your treasured stories and examples are transferred from your chest to your head.

Your treasure chest may become full of situations where your company has helped solve clients' problems. You want to make sure you gather together all the relevant details so that you can present your stories and examples in a credible, factual and captivating way.

In some conversations people naturally remember examples that just pop into their heads and decide to tell some stories on the spur of the moment. But when utilizing them in important professional conversations, it is highly advantageous to have gathered the exact details carefully and to have worked out how to convey them in advance.

Sometimes those who don't do this blurt out what serves as an ill-chosen story, which doesn't effectively back up their message – or a potentially good example that shows up a factual hole in their knowledge about it. Doing this can rebound on your credibility.

So fill your chest with examples and stories where you can get all the relevant facts and are familiar enough with each piece of treasure to know how it can best be deployed.

A good example can sometimes be put forward with a few words or in a single sentence. A good story can sometimes be told in just several sentences. It can be advantageous to have a short version and a longer version – so you have a choice depending on the situation.

Using stories to grab and wow your audience

In a career of journalism, working life is about telling stories with a purpose – to grab the attention of your audience, enlighten them about what is going on and what they need to know and, where possible, make them go "wow" or "aha" or "oh no" or "aw". This should ensure they keep buying your newspaper, reading your blog or tuning in to your news broadcasts and webcasts.

When it comes to selecting the right stories for your treasure chest, there are guidelines that you can borrow from the world of journalism, where one of the essential skills is to be able to spot what makes a great story.

The guiding principle underlying this is "TRUTH". And yes, just as journalists can get into trouble with ethics committees and the law if their stories aren't based on fact, you too need to make sure you have enough facts to convey the real truth. It defeats the whole purpose if you don't.

But in truth, "TRUTH" is also an acronym that outlines the kind of things that a story needs if it's to make an impact. The TRUTH test can help you decide what goes in and what stays out of your treasure chest.

Here's what TRUTH stands for:

T = Topical. Your example or story doesn't have to be brand-spanking new; though as in journalism, it's always great if it is. But it has to be one where the telling of it makes sense at the time it's being conveyed. So it could be a successful case study that your company was involved in some years ago, providing you can make clear that the results are still valid and important at the time you are including it in your answer. If the case study runs past its sell-by date and is no longer significant to the latest developments, then ruthlessly toss it out of your treasure chest and replace it with a new one.

R = Relevant. Your illustration has to be relevant to the particular audience with whom you are conversing. So telling the story or outlining the example needs to be done in such a way that the point of using it makes sense to your particular listeners. It can also be fitting to tell a story that is set geographically close to the audience you are addressing. Most people tend to be more interested in what's happening nearby. A story that has local proximity is bound to have greater impact with your audience in that area.

U = Unusual. In the world of journalism there is a principle that if a dog bites a man – which is, sadly, a fairly common occurrence with man's so-called best friend – it doesn't make it into the news columns. There needs to be something unusual about it for a dog bite to be regarded as news. For example, to make it into the media it needs to be a particularly savage attack or perhaps a bite from a dog owned by a well-known personality. This happened in England when Princess Anne's bull terrier, Dotty, attacked two children. But if a man bites a dog, this would be unusual enough to make news without a big name being involved. Where you can, look for the exceptional story that stands out by being unusual and has the biggest surprise or wow factor. Be aware that sometimes, when looking for the right example, it's beneficial to seek out a typical rather than an extraordinary one. However, you still want to gather enough of the right colourful and fascinating details about it so that it will stick in the audience's mind.

T = Trouble. The media gravitate to controversy and happenings that ruffle society's feathers and more. When choosing examples for your treasure chest, it may be more a case of picking instances where your organization's product or service or insights helped overcome a group's or an individual's brush with some kind of trouble.

H = Human. People love hearing moving stories about people, so the human element in your story is important. In journalism we refer to "human interest" stories as a particular genre. It's the human element that is often where your story can have its biggest impact, by touching the emotions of your audience. So it can be important to show in a success story that what you or your organization did had a positive emotional outcome for one or more people. Tell us if your clients were so overjoyed by what you did for them that they burst into tears – or into song!

To come down the "Ladder of Abstraction" on the TRUTH concept, here's a story that I made up. (Yes, you can justifiably make up stories in some circumstances, but you must tell your audience that's what you are doing!)

This story has been concocted for those I seek to get thinking like journalists. As you need to tell captivating stories in your answers, this now includes you!

This particular story, which I have told variations of around the world, is designed to embrace all the factors that make a scintillating news media story – which means it should grab and hold the attention of your audience.

I'm hoping the story will help you remember the factors that can make it worth putting a particular item in a news bulletin or, in your case, in your treasure chest to utilize in your great answers.

For the purposes of this following exercise, imagine you are a journalist working on a news radio station in City X in Country Y. The question for you at the end is: Is this a story that your listeners need to or want to know about – and if so, why?

The story that hits all factors

There is an ambitious group of nuns who live a quiet existence in a secluded convent just down the road from where we are here in City X. The nuns are campaigning for world peace. They have decided it's their mission to persuade every country in the world to stop exporting weapons. They have figured that if this happens it will be a great way to bring an end to all wars, along with all the associated suffering.

The nuns have been writing to the newspapers and to your radio station to seek publicity for their campaign. But so far no one in the media is taking notice. So today the nuns decide to get radical and grab the media's attention.

Six of the nuns leave their nunnery and walk down to a major highway. When they get there they lift up their habits, kick their legs around like dancing girls and stick out their hitch-hiking thumbs to seek a lift. They quickly attract the attention of a passing truck driver who pulls over to the side of the road.

The peace-campaigning nuns then drag the driver out of his truck, give him a vicious kicking and leave him bleeding beside the road. They climb into the truck and drive to the nearest military base.

When the nuns get to the base they take off their habits and all their other garments and seduce the guards around the perimeter fence. They then grab the guards' guns and race naked onto the base. They point the guns at a group of parading soldiers and a pilot and force them to board a helicopter. Then the nuns order the soldiers to fly the helicopter over the Town Hall of City X.

At this point the chief nun uses one of the soldier's mobile phones to make contact with you at your radio station.

With the helicopter rotors whirring in the background, the chief nun explains who she is and what the nuns have done so far. She corroborates one bit of the story that you had already picked up from elsewhere – about the nuns being spotted cavorting by the roadside and leaving behind a seriously injured truck driver. The chief nun offers to do an interview with your radio station to explain what lies behind their antics.

In the interview the chief nun says the group is demanding that governments around the world agree to sign their declaration to never again export weapons. And they are insisting the prime minister of Country Y immediately announces that he will impose a weapons export ban. The nun also calls upon the actors in Country Y's favourite soap opera to visit the television networks and pledge their support for the cause. And they want the star players in Country Y's national football team to do the same.

Then comes the crunch moment in the interview. The chief nun says that if the prime minister of Country Y does not declare that he will implement the weapons export ban in the next hour, the nuns will push one of the soldiers out of the helicopter and onto the roof of the Town Hall. And if their demands are still not met, ten minutes later they will push out another soldier. She says that every ten minutes after this, if their demands aren't met, an additional soldier will be thrown to his death.

"Eventually", she says, "we will push out the pilot".

"And we are just a bunch of naked nuns who can't fly a helicopter, but we are prepared to die for the cause of world peace because it's so important to everybody on earth!"

Then she hangs up.

So that's the story. Hopefully you agree that it has all the TRUTH factors in it.

It is Topical, as weapons and wars are nearly always prominent in the news these days. This topicality is enhanced by the fact that this unfolding story has drama, is happening now and no one knows how the story will end.

The story is certainly Relevant to your radio station's audience as it could affect their plans for the day and their personal safety. And some of your listeners may well be related to the soldier hostages or to the nuns. The relevance is underlined by the fact that the story is happening around where all your listeners live.

The story is Unusual – because nuns do not normally act in this way. Sometimes my students mistakenly think the story rates as news simply because it contains sex and violence. But sex and violence don't always qualify as news. It's the unusual nature of the sex and violence that count here. The apparent hypocrisy of nuns claiming to be acting for peace but using violence to achieve their ends adds to the newsiness of the story.

The nuns have certainly hit the Trouble factor. It's easy to imagine that the police and perhaps other sections of the armed forces will soon be seeking to intervene to sort out this trouble.

And there is a strong Human element to the story. Newspapers will be wanting to find out the background of the chief nun, write up her history and explore what is driving her. Media researchers will be hunting for details of the lives and loved ones of the hostages. Reporters will be seeking out the soap and football stars the nuns want to support them, to find out what they think. And the prime minister will be under pressure to respond as the media speculate about what he and his government colleagues are going through as they decide how to deal with this situation – and the poor security and easily seduced soldiers around the military base. People like stories about other interesting people, or people in interesting situations, which is why you need to include some of them in your professional conversations.

There is also another factor involved that would fuel journalistic enthusiasm for this story. Despite concerns that terrorists should sometimes not be given the oxygen of publicity, one force driving the media to run this kind of story is what's known in journalism as "public interest" justification. This goes way beyond the fact that the story is seen as merely "interesting to the public". If it's in the public interest to publicize something, it means there is an argument that telling people about the story is a justifiable and necessary thing to do, as your radio listeners will need to know that it's not the right time to do their shopping near the Town Hall in case they get hit by a falling soldier or a crashing helicopter full of naked nuns. Sometimes, in some forums, when addressing tough questions, you may need to expose things and choose particular examples because it's in the public interest – or the interest of that particular audience – for you to do so.

This story about the nuns is designed to touch on all the things that people are interested in – hitting all the TRUTH factors and some more besides. But the good news for you is that your stories or examples don't always need to have every one of the attributes listed here to make it into your treasure chest as a potential illustration to use in your great answers. However, if your illustrations don't have at least one of the factors identified here in each case, then they may not be worthy of inclusion. You want to have stories and examples that shine out for your listeners – and in seeking to ensure this, you will find yourself having much in common with journalists.

Make your stories pass the "So what?" test

One way to test whether your story is captivating enough is with what we call the "So what?" test. You apply this by running through a story you're considering telling, and asking yourself the question "So what?" at key points along the way. If the answer to "So what?" is "Not much" or "No one would really care", then the story is probably not worthy of inclusion in your treasure chest – at least without some modification. Your aim should be to ensure that all the stories in your treasure chest easily pass the "So what?" test. This means they have the potential to capture the imagination of your audience and effectively back up your message.

When the golden formulae for great answers to tough questions are spelled out a little further on, we will look at where to fit your illustrations into your answers. We will also look at how to structure your stories to maximize their impact.

In the meantime, keep gathering those stories and examples for your personal professional treasure chest – and, where appropriate, for your organization's collective treasure chest (start it now if it doesn't already exist). Then you can be well placed to captivate your audiences with your answers – just as those religious leaders and American presidents have long done.

Happy treasure hunting!

Chapter 4

FINDING OUT IN ADVANCE – THEN PLANNING FOR IT

Imagine you are the controller of a space mission about to send your astronauts to boldly go where no human has gone before.

Now zoom back to earth and picture yourself as a general getting ready to assemble your troops around the battlefield for the ultimate showdown with the enemy.

Next transplant yourself into the mind of a children's party organizer on the verge of setting up a picnic birthday celebration for the ten-year-old daughter of your best client and all her excited sisters, brothers and friends.

In each of these situations, as the main planner of a happening that's important – and potentially fraught – there is something you want to have in advance.

You want to get as much knowledge as you can ahead of each situation before the action starts.

As the space mission controller you want to know what conditions are like on the surface of the planet your astronauts will be landing on to avoid the risk of their spaceship getting stuck in a crater full of cosmic quicksand or worse.

As the general you want know how many enemy troops you're facing, what weapons they've got and what their morale is like.

As the children's party organizer you want a dependable weather forecast so you know if it's going to rain and if there's a need to set up a giant tent.

When you're going into a vital conversation that's critical to your career or the future of your organization it's exactly the same.

You want to get ahead in the game by finding out as much about the situation in advance as you can.

This enables you do some planning, preparation and practice.

It may seem obvious, but many people don't do this. They allow themselves to get rushed into a critical conversation without knowing what they're heading into - and not giving themselves a chance to properly think about it in advance.

Don't allow yourself to fall into this trap.

However brilliant you may be, you will always be better with the benefit of some focused thinking time.

The golden rule is, if at all possible, never allow yourself to be rushed into a challenging professional conversation without the chance of knowing what it's about in advance and doing some preparation.

Getting it right in that set-up discussion

The most common way of getting the right intelligence upon which to plan is in the set-up discussion that typically takes place in order to line up what we'll call the big conversation.

The trick is to think ahead when someone is approaching you to arrange that big conversation and get an idea of what territory you might be heading for.

It could be when a PA calls to tell you the boss wants to see you about something serious. There's a massive difference between the boss wanting to pick your brains about that slump in sales figures that he may regard as your fault, and to him seeking your view on how to celebrate the latest award your team has won due to your inspired design skills.

Either way, allowing yourself the chance to discover the agenda in advance and build in a bit of thinking time to plan your responses is a plus.

Saying "No" to this kind of meeting probably isn't a serious option, but before you agree to the exact timing there are still things you can do to get the information you need.

It's potentially more challenging to take control when the person who wants to have the big conversation is actually lining it up with you personally. This is because it's so easy to slide into having the actual conversation there and then – when you have no chance to do any thinking or planning.

The key to success here involves separating the pre-conversation-discussion with the actual big conversation itself. If it's something small, simple and uncontentious then going straight into the conversation there and then may be fine and practical. On a big tough topic where there will be big tough questions it's different. This is where strictly separating the set-up the discussion from the actual big conversation itself is supremely helpful to you. It may also benefit your big conversation partner as they will hopefully gain from your better-planned answers.

In that pre-conversation discussion the foundations to success lie in asking questions – and not getting drawn into answering any tough questions then and there. It may not feel it at the time, but you can be in a strong position to insist on this when it's someone contacting you to line up a meeting with you. If necessary you can present the short time delay as being in their interest for you to go into the big conversation having done your homework.

Also keep in mind the person calling wants something from you. They want a time to have your full attention. And people who want something are usually prepared to give a little bit in return for increasing their chances of getting it – especially if it's just information they have to surrender in order to achieve what they want.

Remember at the time of the pre-conversation discussion, you have some power. You can potentially say "Yes" or "No" or "Please tell me more". My advice is to use the power wisely and immediately when you have it – before you've agreed to anything.

But you can do so in a subtle and sophisticated way. My suggested starting point is, if it's feasible, to signal a general willingness for agreeing to what they want without immediately signing up to the details. You can agree in principle that you will come and have that meeting with the boss to instantly demonstrate you are being co-operative – even if it is something which in reality that you don't have a lot of choice over. But you may not have to agree to arranging the exact time until you've found out more about what will be required of you at the meeting.

I recommend that if the topic isn't immediately made obvious you say something like "Please tell me more about what you would like on the agenda." In most cases they will probably tell you more just out of a desire to be helpful. But because they need something – a date and time in the diary – then they have an incentive to tell you more.

The real trick to getting it right in this delicate phase of the pre-conversation dance, lies in a children's game I used to enjoy in Australia called "Yes, No Jackpots". In this game you have a conversation with your opponent where you take it in turns to talk.

The winner is the one who avoids saying "Yes" or "No" during the conversation. The easiest way to win is to restrict yourself to only asking questions at key points in the discussion.

Asking the right questions, so you can prepare the right answers

By only asking questions in the preliminary chat phase you can avoid giving badly composed off-the-top-of-your-head answers on the run. And you can simultaneously be building your knowledge of the situation so you're in a better position to give great answers when the time is right.

So the kind of questions you need to be asking can be:

- What is the person initiating the meeting most concerned about or most interested in?
- Is there anything else they want to discuss?
- Who else will be taking part in the conversation?
- Is there anything you would like me to prepare in advance?

When you have got all the information you require, make sure you allow enough time to do your planning for it when agreeing to the timing of the meeting.

Then of course you need to do the planning. Even a few minutes is so much more valuable than no planning at all.

Having a pro-active and reactive plan

In planning for important professional conversations, you typically want to have a pro-active plan and a reactive plan to deal with questions.

The pro-active plan involves having great messages and illustrations ready for where you can and should be getting across initial positive points. The reactive plan is your insurance policy readying you for tough questions that could conceivably be asked.

So if you were planning for a conversation with medical regulators about a new drug being launched then the pro-active plan would concern messages and examples about the benefits of the drug – what it could cure and how effective it is. The reactive plan would concern any potential downside of the drug, so it could involve details about trials done to test for side-effects and what safety precautions are in place.

When you have both a combined pro-active and reactive plan, consider yourself close to being prepared.

Here's some guidance on how to use your well-earned preparation time to efficiently get together what you need.

Getting your preparation right

Depending on how religious you are, you may think that with the meeting in your diary now is the time to say a prayer!

But whatever your religious preferences, a valuable approach to effective rapid preparation is based on what's called the "AMEN" concept.

This enables you to focus on what you need to work through in advance.

As you read through the details of the AMEN formula, you may find it useful – even therapeutic – to apply it to a specific tough negative topic relating to your work that you could be being asked about. By doing this you will get some useful practice at starting to prepare for your next challenging conversation on this subject.

Here's what AMEN stands for:

A = Audience. Whether you are dealing with a one-to-one conversation or a larger gathering, always identify your audience and focus your preparations on what they require. And if you don't know the make-up or thinking of your audience – if it's for answering questions as part of a presentation for a new client, for example – then do a little research to find out.

M = Messages. You'll recall from earlier chapters, your encounter is an opportunity to get across your messages. So work out your headline message – and any additional messages you wish to convey as part of your pro-active and reactive plans.

E = Examples. Pick out examples and/or real life stories from your treasure chest that back up each of your messages most effectively for that particular audience, so you can come down that Ladder of Abstraction and bring them alive in the minds of your listeners.

N = Negatives. Write down all the negative questions that could be thrown at you. This is the key part of your reactive plan. Don't hold back here. Phrase the negative questions in the toughest, most ferocious way you can. In reality the questions you actually get may well turn out not be worded as nastily as you phrase them. But the principle here is use the same approach that many effective sports coaches deploy when preparing their team for a tough contest: "Train hard, and play easy." So if you train for the harshest conditions, when it comes to the reality of playing the game for real it will probably be easier for you than it was in training – and you should perform all the better as a result.

Turning a negative mindset to a positive one

It is the negative questions that naturally make people the most nervous about tough conversations. So let's now focus on this area so you can get yourself into the best possible shape to deal with them. This is vital for your confidence and for developing the winning mindset you will need if you are to come out of your encounters in the best possible way.

This next bit is seriously uplifting.

It's designed to get you into a positive frame of mind – whether you like it or not!

Now it's important at this point that you don't focus on the actual wording of the answers you will give. We will deal with these when you learn the golden formulae over the next two chapters. At the moment we are just dealing with the early phase of preparation.

What you do at this stage is write down things that will force you to focus in a realistically positive manner.

Next to each negative question contemplate, not the answer, but something else.

Write down *THE BEST THINGS YOU CAN SAY ON THIS TOPIC!*

This is in capitals and italics to underline its importance.

The technique is designed to get you to be and feel supremely positive – however intimidating the question.

So your question from a disgruntled customer could be something like:

Why did the product you sold us break in the first five minutes of us using it?

Now it may well be appropriate that you express sympathy and probably apologize at the start of your answer, but we will deal with this in forthcoming chapters.

You will also need to formulate a positive headline message to sum up your approach.

It may be something like: "On rare occasions when something goes wrong with our products we make sure it's rectified as soon as possible, that the customer is given an extra bonus as compensation and that we learn any lessons from what happened to ensure our products are constantly being improved."

The "best things you can say" list needs to be in line with this headline message.

This headline message, combined with the "best things you can say" list, helps you to magically get into the right positive mindset to deal with the tough issue and gives you supremely useful material to inject into the conversation.

So in your list of "best things you can say" you can include points such as:

- We have a policy of immediately replacing any product that proves less than perfect – and also giving the affected customer a high value gift certificate as a goodwill gesture

- Tests and surveys have shown that the products that break in the first year of use are less than one in ten-thousand

- In the unusual event of a product breaking we ensure it is examined by our laboratory so that we can work out what has occurred and how best to prevent the same thing from happening again in the future

- We have a quality control team which is constantly looking at our processes to ensure there is focus on continual improvement on our systems and products.

So even though something undesirable has happened, there are still lots of potentially positive things that you can say that are in the interests of the customer with the broken product – and other customers and potential buyers – to hear.

Can you feel relief and even a sensation of being uplifted when you allow yourself to acknowledge these positives?

Apply the "best things you can say" approach to your preparation to face all your tough questions.

This list of "best things" will be supremely useful when you are putting together just the right elements to deploy in your great answers.

This list can make you feel better about whatever questions you face – and help equip you with the winning mentality that you need for success.

Chapter 5

THE FIRST GOLDEN FORMULA – SIMPLE AS ABCDE

Let's assume you've found out in advance what you can about an approaching situation involving anticipated tough questions.

You have worked out what those questions are likely to be.

You've also prepared your list of "best things you can say" for each of these questions. This is already helping put you in a more positive frame of mind.

Now comes the crunch.

When you're asked a tough question, your standard practice at the start of your reply is something that takes a lot of people by surprise.

You need to get straight to the point, tell the truth and actually answer it if you possibly can.

How you structure your answer is critical

Exactly *how* you actually convey this truth as part of the whole of your answer is the critical thing.

And here's the supremely important bit.

While giving the appropriate factual information in your answer, you need to make sure you ALSO convey something extra.

The extra something you must add is a crucial positive message.

This positive message has to be related to the question – so it's effectively providing an additional benefit for your audience.

This positive message should be inspired by and in harmony with your list of "best things you can say".

It's this positive message that helps you to hit that win/win target between you and your listeners – to give them the response they seek AND something else that's really useful besides.

In order to respond to the question in a way that is simultaneously bombproof and impressive, you need to know something really important: how to structure your answer.

This is where you need what I call The First Golden Formula for giving great answers to tough questions.

When you grasp this structure you'll see it's simultaneously logical and inspirational – and is helpful to both you and your audience.

But the structure is not something the typical human brain seems to work out intuitively for itself.

When you're shown it in a moment you will hopefully recognize its power, simplicity and magic.

But there are vital things to understand first.

Deal with the bad – then gravitate to the positive

Fundamental to the formula is that if the question relates to bad things that have happened or could happen, these typically need to be addressed.

The First Golden Formula involves speaking exact truths that will stand up to robust scrutiny.

However, you can do this in a way that helps your questioner. You may enable them to view the situation in a wider context.

Or you may show them helpful things that are beyond the confines of their question.

And you need to do it in such a way that you are saying what should be said, rather than allowing yourself to be a mere slave to any limitations in their question.

It's important to understand that simply addressing the challenging aspect of the question is not enough to constitute a truly great answer.

Central to your great answer is the premise that once you have dealt with any bad stuff, you are then entitled to gravitate to the positive and say that something extra.

For example, the positive may well include saying what you are doing about the bad stuff in order to put things right.

The key thing to remember is this: *Once you have given the initially requested response, then you are perfectly entitled – sometimes even duty bound – to convey a positive message that will be in the interests of your listeners.*

Naturally you want to be helpful to your questioner and to any wider audience.

Once you have given that vital requested information at the start of your reply, you have – under the normal rules of conversation – earned a kind of licence to say a bit more.

So what do you add?

Something based on one of the best things you can say.

It is dealing with the negative and getting across a positive message that enables you to land in that win/win zone for you and your audience.

The First Golden Formula enables you to do this.

Which is why it is indeed a "golden formula".

In simple, memorable terms The First Golden Formula is as simple as: ABCDE.

Hopefully you will find this easy to remember.

So here's what it stands for – and the route you will take when deploying it.

A = answer or acknowledge the question
If you know the answer and are allowed to give it out, then do so upfront.

Getting this right is known as being the opposite of sex.

Why?

Because unlike sex, when you structure your answer properly the climactic moment comes at the start!

But what about when you don't know the answer – or for some legitimate reason you are under constraints not to disclose the answer?

In this case the formula changes.

If you can't reveal what the answer is, then:

A = Acknowledge

You acknowledge openly that you can't answer it.

The crucial thing here is to immediately explain WHY you can't answer it.

If you briefly give the reason why you don't know the answer, or why you're not allowed to give it out, then this can instantaneously take the pressure out of what can otherwise be a tense situation.

Often there is an excellent reason for not knowing or not disclosing.

For example, you may not know because your research team is still working to find out what the answer is. So say so!

And – if practical and appropriate – explain that you will let the questioner know what the answer is as soon as you discover it. Make sure you follow through on this, because your credibility is on the line here.

But in some cases you may not be allowed to give out an answer for a very good reason. It could be on legal grounds, so as not to prejudice the course of justice in a forthcoming trial. So say so!

Perhaps you can't reveal the details because you need to protect the confidentiality of a client. So say so!

In some cases, such as when dealing with military or crime-fighting matters, it could even be because lives may be put at risk by giving out the information. Or you may need to keep a commercial secret. So say so!

This is an area that causes so many people so much grief, simply because they don't say why they can't reply. So they stumble, mutter, sweat, get embarrassed, look guilty, feel guilty and worse.

It can be remarkably liberating when you explain why you can't answer, as both you and your audience typically feel better about the situation because of this shared understanding.

But the key thing to know – as far as your well-structured answer is concerned – is that when you have answered the question or acknowledged why you can't or won't answer it, YOU DON'T JUST LEAVE IT THERE.

At this point you have given the start of a great answer, but giving a truthful, factual response upfront is typically just the beginning.

You must move things on – so that you kick that goal or hit that home run with your answer.

B = crossing the bridge to the positive

The key to moving it on from here is B:

B = Bridge

A "bridge" in this context is a verbal tool that, having dealt with the question in your initial response, or acknowledged why you can't, enables you to move things on to a more productive and useful space.

A typical bridge is:

- "What's really important is…"

- "What everyone needs to understand is…"

- "To put the situation in a wider context…"

- "But…" (a supremely simple bridge)

- "And…" (another simple bridge – and potentially a positive one)

The crucial thing is that, having dealt with any bad stuff in A, you must then use B to enable you to verbally cross over onto positive territory.

That leads on to C.

C = get across the content of your message (which is typically positive)

Once you have crossed the bridge, this is the time to convey your positive content.

Given that you typically have a number of positive messages you need to get across – inspired by your list of "best things you can say" – you need to select the message that relates most closely to the question.

It could be your headline message, or it could be one of your other support messages.

Sometimes you say this message overtly.

At other times you word things in a form that's different from how you phrased the message while preparing, but in a way that gets your message across nonetheless.

At this point you have effectively scored.

You have kicked that goal in football or hit that home run in baseball.

However, at this stage in your response there's still more that can be done and *should* be done to make your answer complete.

In a game of rugby or American football, when you score a try or a touchdown, you then get a chance to have a bonus kick at goal to potentially gain extra points. If you succeed in kicking this goal, it's what these codes call "a conversion".

So in your answer, when you get to C and you have conveyed the content of your message, then you too have a chance to effectively earn extra points and "convert" your answer into a total success.

Here's how.

D + E = dangle an example

You now have the opportunity to make your answer even more engaging, more meaningful and more memorable.

To do this you move to D and E, which go together:

D = Dangle

E = Example

When you have conveyed your message and delivered the content of your key message, you then "dangle" an "example".

The dangle is like another bridge. It's a verbal tool that enables you to move smoothly into giving an example to bring alive what you mean in your audience's mind with an illustration.

So, a typical dangle is something like this: "A really good example of what I'm saying is…" or "Let me tell you a story about how it once worked in the past…"

The dangle inherently flags up that what is about to be said is important or fascinating – or hopefully both.

You use a dangle just as you might display a bunch of carrots in front of a colony of rabbits to arouse their interest.

Then you move to E and give your example. Or it could be a story. Or it could be an analogy that helps illuminate your message.

This is where you come down that "Ladder of Abstraction" (see Chapter 3) to paint a picture in the minds of your audience so they can literally see what you mean.

So, you conclude your great answer with your example, story or other form of illustration.

One of the advantages of this is that your illustration is typically positive – and so finishing your answer at the end of your illustration is a positive place to finish.

People often struggle to know when to finish their answers. Ending on the example enables you to conclude crisply and decisively on a high.

There's more on how to structure your examples and stories coming up in Chapter 7.

But the vital thing to grasp for the moment is that when you have finished your example or story you stop – just as you would when you deliver the punchline of a joke.

Your example or story doesn't have to be funny – it can be quite the opposite. But it gives you a chance to draw your answer to a clear-cut and authoritative ending.

And that's what you do and keep doing every time you get a tough question.

So when you have worked through the ABCDE formula in an answer you have ideally given the questioners the information needed, conveyed your positive message and captivated them with a picture in their minds that they can take away to remember later.

If they ask you another tough question, which they sometimes do, you go through the ABCDE formula again – this time ending, for the sake of variety, with a different example.

Extra advantages of ending on your example

There are two additional benefits to ending your well-structured reply on an example or a story.

Assuming it's a positive illustration, this often prompts a positive follow-up question.

If you tell a story about how someone followed your organization's advice and benefited hugely as a result, it's likely to prod a question along the lines of: "Could that happen for me too?"

When you are effectively dictating the next question, you are typically doing well in a professional conversation. We'll explore this concept further at the end of this chapter.

Ending on a positive example or story also stops you doing what many people have a tendency to do – and that's to cross back over the bridge into the negative territory, which was instigated by a negative question at the outset.

The idea of successful bridging is that you only cross the bridge after you have dealt with the negative. Once you cross the bridge you are in the positive zone of your positive message, which then leads on to your typically positive example or story.

So, once you have bridged into the positive zone, you don't want to cross back over the bridge into the negative zone. Those who do are effectively asking for a metaphorical slap, as crossing back into the negative makes it so much easier for your questioner to ask you another uncomfortable negative question.

Regard the bridge as being a one-way bridge and, once you've crossed it, stay on the sunlit uplands of the positive territory on the other side of the river.

Making the formula work for you

So, let's look at how the ABCDE formula can work in practice.

For the purposes of the exercise, assume you have been employed as a trainee sales representative in a firm over the past year and are due for your first annual appraisal. In your view and in the opinion of most of your colleagues who you've discussed your progress with, things have gone very well overall. You have met your monthly sales targets in 11 of the first 12 months.

However, two customers have complained to your company that you got their orders wrong because, having sealed the deal, you filled in a few details incorrectly on their order forms. You did ensure they got the right orders in the end, and you have recognized that your attention to detail needs improving. Having sought advice from your colleagues, when completing order forms you now routinely get your customers to check over what's been written to make sure what is recorded is exactly what they require.

Meanwhile, you are having some success in generating new customers for the firm by seeking out contacts in industries that your company hasn't tapped into before.

However, let's also surmise that you have a jealous senior colleague who has recently written an unfair assessment about your performance – greatly exaggerating the problems caused on your order forms.

So, you need to prepare for a question from your line manager such as: "Isn't it fair to say that your performance has been poor largely because of your lack of attention to detail, as underlined by those complaints from two customers, which indicates you are not suited to being a sales rep?"

This is a toughly worded question, harder than most people face during a typical appraisal.

But in the spirit of "train hard, play easy", let's tackle it.

We can start by compiling that list of "the best things you can say". These include:

- You have nearly always hit your monthly sales targets.

- The majority of your customers are happy with what you've been doing over the past year.

- Most of your colleagues who you have discussed your performance with believe you are making very good progress.

- You are working at overcoming your challenge of needing to pay more attention to detail, and with the help of colleagues you have worked out a way to tackle it which is proving effective.

- You have successfully been exploring new avenues for sales in other industries.

So based on this, your overall headline message could be:

> *"My progress as a sales rep has been going very well and I have worked out ways to perform even better for the company in the future."*

Now let's apply the ABCDE formula to that horrid question which, to remind you, is:

> *"Isn't it fair to say that your performance has been poor largely because of your lack of attention to detail, as underlined by those complaints from two customers, which indicates you are not well-suited to being a sales rep?"*

A: "No, it isn't. Overall progress has been going very well, which is underlined by the fact that I have met my monthly sales targets in 11 out of the first 12 months and the overwhelming majority of my customers say they're very happy with my service."

B: "And what's really important is that I have found ways I can take my performance to a higher level in future."

C: "With the help of my colleagues, who have been very positive about my progress, I have a way of guaranteeing that the order forms are correctly completed by ensuring that I always check them over with the client before they are lodged. I now pass this tip on to new people joining the team. And I have been growing the market for the company by successfully exploring new avenues for sales in industries where we haven't previously been active."

D: "The best example of this is…"

E: "I have built up contacts in the mobile phone industry by using social media and have now been making sales to XYZ Mobiles. This has been so successful that I'm in discussions about what could turn out to be one of the biggest orders in our company's history, valued at over £200,000 a year."

So what's been achieved with this draft answer?

You have decisively yet calmly tackled the proposed unfair assessment head-on at the start and provided immediate evidence to refute it.

Showing humility, but without running yourself down unnecessarily, you have frankly acknowledged that your attention to detail can be better and you have indicated how you are succeeding in improving this.

You've conveyed a message that your performance is likely to be even better in the future.

You have illustrated how this could be the case.

You've successfully come down the "Ladder of Abstraction" and dangled a big future opportunity for the company, which has been unearthed due to your initiative, so giving a powerful incentive for the company to keep you on in your sales rep role.

You may well also have headed off further questions based on the unfair report by your jealous colleague, and at the very least, have made it more difficult for such questions to be asked again in a credible way.

You've wisely avoided specifically mentioning the jealous colleague and the unfair assessment, so you have not put it on the agenda yourself.

You have made helpful references to your colleagues in general and, in referring to seeking their advice, positioned yourself as someone who doesn't pretend to have all the answers yourself and is using the wisdom and experience of colleagues to help advance your performance for the benefit of the company. You've also given evidence that you are a good team player by passing on helpful advice you have received to others.

You still have other things from your list of "best things you can say," which you can potentially deploy if the topic of the unfair report is raised directly.

Phrasing answers with your positive words

Having revealed The First Golden Formula and seen how it works, there are a few associated tips and variations of it which can be useful.

The first of these concerns the language you use.

It's very common for tough questions to be loaded with one or more negative words.

One of the important principles in wording your replies is to make sure you don't unnecessarily echo back these negative words.

Repeating negatives ensures that you generate a negative impression, and also traps your performance within the unhelpful vocabulary of your questioner.

You certainly need to respond effectively to any negative words underpinning negative questions, but the trick is to do so in such a way that you control the language.

Your aspiration should be to say what you want to say in words that are as positive as circumstances allow.

Words have power, and you want to pick your words judiciously to avoid being trapped unfairly by nasty ones.

There is one particularly big reason why you don't want to echo back negative words, even if you are denying that they are accurate in the situation you are discussing.

When in conversation, the human brain isn't very good at dealing with the concept of "not" in front of a negative.

So, repeating a negative word while putting "not" before it tends to reinforce the negative concept in the minds of your listeners.

For example, you will create an unfortunate impression if you respond to an accusation about your organization's services being "hopeless, useless and a waste of money" by saying "Our services are not hopeless, not useless and not a waste of money".

Even though what you are saying is hopefully perfectly accurate, the wording encourages the brain to focus on those powerful negatives.

So, if you phrase your reply in terms of being "not hopeless", "not useless" and "not a waste of money", it is those negative concepts precisely that stick in the minds of your listeners and taint your organization in the process.

How to avoid echoing negatives

One way to avoid echoing back negatives is to use something called a "blocking phrase".

This means that you start your answer with something that instantly deadens the power of the negative words being used against you.

Where the truth allows, your blocking phrase can be a denial.

So you can simply say: "That's not the case."

In other situations, which may be less clear-cut, a straight denial may not be justifiable or credible.

In these instances you can use a more neutral blocking phrase, such as: "Let me put it like this…"

Whenever negative words are thrown at you in a question, your blocking phrase should be used at the start of "A" in The First Golden Formula.

Having blocked the force of the negative words without repeating them, you should then go on to say what you want to say in your positive words.

So, it could be something like: "Independent assessments have shown that our services rate as very effective, highly competent and great value."

To capitalize on the power of your words, you want to accurately select positive words to convey the right positive impression.

Using a blocking phrase and then carefully selecting the right positive words to follow it puts you in charge of your answer and of making a favourable impression.

This technique also stops you inadvertently buying into a false premise, and allows you to positively reframe a situation to your advantage.

Moving from the specific to the general

There is another rule that's also valuable when utilizing the ABCDE formula.

This applies to a situation where you are asked about something very specific, which you don't know much about – or something where it may be unwise to go into detail.

What you can do in these circumstances is apply a rule called "The Specific to the General".

Suppose something is mentioned to you in a preamble to a question, which you haven't had the opportunity to verify – or a question is asked about a situation that you are not free to discuss.

Having explained why you can't deal with it directly, what can be helpful here is for you to talk in more general terms about the policy that your organization follows when it comes to dealing with the kind of specific that is being asked about.

So, you can say something like: "I'm unable to talk about the details of this situation because of advice from our lawyers, but what I can say is that the key principles we follow when faced with this kind of situation are…"

Here, the first part about being unable to talk about the details is your "A" for acknowledge, the "B" for bridge is "but what I can say is…" and the rest of it will be your "C" for the content of your message.

As you can't talk about specifics here, you may not be able to use the "D" for dangle or "E" for example part of the formula.

The formula you are therefore using is effectively just "ABC", which takes you from dealing with the specific you can't go into and from there onto the helpful, more general message that you can convey.

Moving from the general to the specific

There is another rule that is equally helpful when you need to move your answer in the opposite direction.

This rule helps you shift the focus from a general situation that may be difficult to talk about onto a specific aspect of it that you may be much better equipped to discuss.

Hence this rule is called – as you can possibly guess – "The General to the Specific".

It's particularly useful when you are asked about a general area that is outside your zone of expertise and about which you may not know very much.

But you may know about one specific example related to the area – and this is an opportunity for you to help your listener by giving something rather than nothing.

So your answer can be framed something like: "This question relates to a subject which is outside my zone of expertise, but what I can tell you about is one particular instance in that area where we achieved a very positive outcome which was…"

Here you are effectively following the ABCDE formula and hitting the win/win territory between you and your audience by focusing on something useful you can share with them.

Dictating that next question

The better you are doing with your answers, the more control you will have over the direction of the whole conversation.

So, getting your great messages and powerful illustrations out in each of your answers at or near the start of the conversation can have a very strong influence on how the rest of it unfolds and what is concluded by your audience.

The more powerfully you make your case in your answers, the less questioners will normally be inclined to ask you tough questions – because if a tough question is not justified by what has led up to it, then this can effectively backfire on the asker.

A questioner will normally be aware of this – especially if there are others witnessing your conversation – either present in the room or linked via technology.

Hence, one of the things you can strive for in really mastering the art of handling tough conversations is to make sure your answers positively influence what is discussed next and how it is discussed.

A very effective way of doing this is with a variation of The First Golden Formula known as "ABCD".

This kind of reply ends on the dangle but stops short of giving the normal example.

If you play your cards right here, what you'll find is that you effectively force your questioner to ask you for the example you have carefully held back.

This formula works well when you have something you know will be really enticing for your audience.

Let's suppose it's a report that your organization has just completed about a really juicy topic that will be of interest to a potential client because they have big problems in this particular area and the report contains some cutting-edge solutions. It has been cleared for publication, but hasn't yet been released. You can therefore talk about it for the first time.

So, you can flag up the report during the conversation as you are going through the ABCD sequence.

You can then end on a dangle like: "Our organization has just completed a report which for the first time reveals the details of how this kind of problem will be solved more effectively in the very near future with some of the new methods we are developing that are truly amazing."

So what will a typical questioner do next?

They will probably almost beg you to tell them more, by saying something like: "Can you please tell me what these new methods are?"

In this way you are effectively taking control of the conversation, not just through your answers but by influencing the questions as well.

Who's in charge now?

And is this empowering or what?

Chapter 6

THE SECOND GOLDEN FORMULA – WHAT TO SAY WHEN SOMETHING GOES SERIOUSLY WRONG

If you've been inspired by how The First Golden Formula can put you in a positive frame of mind and help you tackle so many of those tough questions that the workplace can throw at you, then that's splendid.

But before you get too swept away by the amazing usefulness and power of the formula, it's necessary to give you a gentle warning at this point.

There are some tough questions where the ABCDE approach is not the best available – especially with your first answer in an emotionally charged professional conversation.

The ABCDE formula has its limitations in situations where something has gone seriously wrong – and where your questioners and any audience beyond are likely to be deeply upset.

This chapter outlines The Second Golden Formula, which is generally preferable when it comes to highly emotive questions, such as:

- Why didn't you have higher safety standards to prevent my child being killed on this dangerous school trip?

- How on earth did you manage to infuriate our biggest client so much that he's threatening to close his account with us?

- Why don't you admit that it's your company's product that has made my lovely kitten Tiddles so ill and suffer so much pain?

The key thing with these questions, where something very serious has happened, is that the person asking them is probably experiencing emotional pain.

And to pile the pressure on you, they often shape their question to implicitly suggest that you are to blame – or are at least the prime suspect.

Whatever the facts of each individual case, which you may or may not be aware of at the time you get the question, the vital thing to do first is recognize and respond to this emotional pain.

Until you engage with this, the questioner is not likely to be able to focus clearly or objectively on the rational side of dealing with what has happened.

So you need to connect with their emotional side and show that you care about them *before* you can move onto the more factual side of your answer.

Talk to the heart before the head

When emotions run high, respond to the heart before you talk to the head.

You know yourself that when something has just happened that has upset you, it can be difficult to immediately deal logically with the practical side of the matter.

That is why the ABCDE formula isn't the ideal starting point for a first answer when the questioner is distraught.

It's as if dealing logically with a question through the ABCDE formula is too clinical for someone in a deeply emotional state.

Let's examine why.

Take an extreme case, where somebody has been accidentally killed on the premises where you work – something that will hopefully never happen during your career, but which it is wise to be ready for.

A tearful relative of the deceased could ask you, if you have a position of authority: "Will you resign because the lax safety standards on the premises led to the death of my son Fred today?"

At this point you and others are probably seeking to both gather the facts about the situation and actually start to deal with the surrounding tasks and challenges.

You would, quite understandably, be battling with the emotional impact of what's happened yourself.

Answering the resignation question in line with the ABCDE formula and starting off with a "Yes", "No" or "It's too early to make a decision owing to…" would be wrong.

This is because it would seem callous and inappropriate for you to be engaging directly on a question about your future at a time of tragedy for your questioner, even though it's your questioner who has raised the subject.

So when something has gone seriously wrong, you need to use The Second Golden Formula that immediately allows you to deal with the emotions involved before moving on.

And here it is…

The formula is called "CARE" and reflects the fact that you do, of course, care about the emotional pain of the questioner, regardless of the rights and wrongs of any accusations they may throw at you.

You need to be caring and rightly perceived as caring – however unfair or even illogical their questions may seem at the time.

Show your concern right at the start

Here's what CARE stands for.

C = concern
You need to address the emotional aspect of the situation right at the outset – even in preference to giving a direct answer to the question.

To do anything else can be perceived as unfeeling, and potentially almost inhuman.

Using the actual word "concern" early on may be helpful in many cases.

In extreme situations, such as those involving a death or injury, then it may even be reasonable to judiciously use the word "sorry".

When an apology is required, then saying "sorry" *at the appropriate time* in a direct and sincere way can have a beneficial effect and be the right thing to do.

It can put you and your organization in the correct position morally, take the sting out of a situation and prepare the way for you to move on to positively address the issues involved.

However, you do need to be extremely careful in the very early stages as you don't want to be appearing to accept liability for a situation that isn't clear, especially when you haven't had legal or other relevant professional advice.

The opinion of lawyers and other outside professionals can be vital in serious situations. But giving a full, official, legally approved apology for something would normally require their involvement and takes time to organize and get signed off.

The key principle in the immediate aftermath of something going wrong is not to let anything unnecessary get in the way of making simple, humane, non-official verbal gestures early on at a time when your questioners are struggling to come to grips with bad news.

In circumstances like the one we are discussing here, you should reasonably and sincerely be able to say something like: "I'm so sorry about the death of your son…"

You may even, with great caution, use the word "sorry" in a situation where you have been falsely accused of doing something that has caused emotional distress.

For example, you can say: "I'm really sorry that you are feeling this way…"

The guiding principle is that no one can expect the conversation to develop constructively until the feelings of an emotionally distraught questioner are openly acknowledged.

Some well-chosen words touching on the emotions at the start are vital. As those philosophers on human feelings, the Bee Gees, sang: "It's only words, and words are all I have…"

But of course, however heartfelt and sincerely expressed, your initial statement of concern consists only of words, albeit very important ones.

So whatever the situation, you have to follow up your words of concern with the next step of the formula.

A = action
You can't just talk emptily, in isolation from reality in an emotionally charged situation.

You need to show signs of doing something appropriate to back up your stated concern.

So whatever has distressed your questioner, you need to identify what is being done – or what will be done.

In the early stages, when a tragedy has just come to light, this could involve simply learning more about it.

So the action line could be: "We are doing everything we can to find out more about what led to this situation..."

It might also include: "We will fully co-operate with the authorities and with any public inquiry to help discover exactly what happened."

And if it's before you have had the chance to put together a "to do" list in response to the situation, the action line could contain: "We are planning to call together all the people who work in this area to determine what we need to do."

One of the challenging things when you've been put in the spotlight over something that has gone wrong is what to say when there is very little you can realistically and safely say.

The point here is that you need to be *doing* something – and saying something about what you are doing.

Expressions that just don't work, and can infuriate your questioners, are "There is nothing we can do" or "No comment" or "We don't know what to do".

Saying that you are working out what to do is so much better than any of these lines, and is commendable for its simple honesty and openness.

Where possible, always – at the very least – indicate what you are doing in order to establish what it is you actually need to do.

Doing nothing and saying nothing is not an option when something has gone seriously wrong.

At the heart of the challenge, when something terrible has happened, is to take a responsible attitude and demonstrate it.

This does not necessarily mean taking actual responsibility for the cause of what has happened if that's not accurate or appropriate or is not yet clear.

It does mean owning the problem, instead of hiding from it.

It means doing helpful things and telling people about them.

R = reassurance

Hopefully you have gathered that dealing effectively with tough questions always involves getting across a message.

And in the case where something has gone seriously wrong, your message needs to be as reassuring as circumstances allow.

Of course, in formulating your message you need to keep in mind the emotional state of your questioner and any other audience members.

Your reassurance may involve several messages depending on what you perceive as the priorities of the moment.

It may be to do with getting things back to normal as quickly and safely as possible.

It could well involve learning from what has happened and using what is gleaned to ensure you do everything possible to minimize the chances of having something like this occur again.

So, your overall reassuring headline message in a situation involving anything serious could be something like:

"We are doing everything we can to make sure those affected are properly supported. And we will do whatever we can to learn any lessons and to take steps to ensure that, as far as possible, something like this can never happen again."

This is one of those messages that you may say overtly – as well as use to guide the thrust of all your conversations relating to the situation.

It is worth refining the wording of your message closely before any conversation – and reviewing it to make sure that everything you say is responsible and can pass the truth test.

So, make sure that you don't actually say something that is unrealistic, like stating baldly: "This will never happen again."

Saying anything that doesn't pass the reasonable credibility test can put you in a situation where you are unbelievable and make yourself a hostage to fortune in the future.

If you say something will never happen again, and it actually does occur, then your reputation will suffer – and you will be reminded in all sorts of ways about the folly of your original statement.

So it is wise to insert what are effectively little caveats to ensure your answer is realistic, such as by saying: "We will do everything we can to *seek to* ensure this will never happen again."

You need to make sure that the fine print of what you are saying will stand up to instant examination and longer-term scrutiny.

Anything you say that is meant to be reassuring, but is overtly not true, is unsettling for your questioners and undermines your credibility at a time when you most need to protect it.

So you need to be realistically reassuring.

You also need to be an inspiring communicator to ensure your audience can effectively picture what you mean.

It is more about show than tell – hence the final part of the CARE formula...

E = example

As with The First Golden Formula, the second one ends on an example to make sure that you are painting the right picture in the minds of your listeners.

You need to come down that "Ladder of Abstraction" outlined in Chapter 3 and give an example of one or more things that you are doing to illustrate your reassuring message.

It may be that to back up your contention that you are doing everything to learn the lessons from the situation you identify the team, or indicate the positions of people, who will be working on this mission.

Be aware that you may also need to come down the ladder earlier with your answer in the "Action" part, in order to illustrate along the way the things that are being implemented or planned.

A useful example or story to end your answer on could relate to a similar crisis that once happened in your organization or another similar one – and where, despite a terrible initial incident, effective steps were taken in response that led to a happier future outcome.

When doing your planning for responses when something has gone seriously wrong, push yourself to think of useful relevant examples and stories.

The right, well-told simple story or example can be easy for your audience to grasp at a time of distress – so it could be the most reassuring and easily remembered part of your answer.

Let's have a look at how the CARE formula can be used in a specific situation.

As we have already touched on dramatic problems involving death and injury, here is a situation where you need to deal with emotions that are running high but where the potential damage is monetary and personal rather than physical.

Using the care approach in action

Let's suppose you are a new sales representative at Company A, reporting to the Sales Director. You have your first meeting with an established client, the Purchasing Officer at Company B. The meeting seems to go well and concludes with you promising to send a requested quote for an additional service they are interested in.

However, when you send the quote, the Purchasing Officer gets very upset. Unbeknown to you, he is used to getting a 15% discount on all services from your company, which your predecessor – a long-serving sales rep who has now retired – was allowed to routinely offer.

The Purchasing Officer, when seeing that he wasn't being offered his regular 15% discount, rings your Managing Director to complain about you not giving the best possible price. He says he is very upset and is considering taking his business to a rival company.

Your Managing Director is furious about a longstanding client being unsettled. He calls in your line manager, the Sales Director, and criticizes the sales department for not being consistent with its discounts. The Managing Director says he is considering dismissing the Sales Director as a result.

The Sales Director talks to his PA and indicates that he thinks it's your fault for not finding out about the standard discount before sending the quote to the client. The PA calls you to come to the Sales Director's office. You correctly ask the right kind of questions and find out what you can expect when you are confronted by him.

It seems you can expect an angry outburst and a question, like: "I'm in danger of losing my job because of you. Why did you infuriate the Purchasing Officer in Company B by failing to offer the standard discount that they are used to and which could lead to you losing us one of our biggest clients?"

Not surprisingly, you don't think the problem can reasonably be blamed on you. But you know that saying "It's not my fault" is not a great answer. So, you work out how you can apply the CARE formula to this question.

Concern: You decide that using the word "sorry" in this context could mistakenly lead to you looking as though you are admitting that the situation is your fault. So you opt for the safer choice of using the word "concern".

Your opening could be: "I am really concerned that you are being put in a difficult position over this and that our Managing Director and the Purchasing Officer are upset." (You would normally use their actual names, rather than titles.)

Action: Having touched on the emotions involved, this is where you can go some way towards actually answering the question.

You need to both deal with this specific situation and suggest something to be done on a wider front to stop this kind of thing from recurring.

You could say: "As a newcomer who wasn't briefed on the whole background about dealings with Company B, I'm very happy to sit down with you and see if we can offer a revised quotation."

Then you can move to the bigger picture.

"It would be really helpful if I could be given the relevant details about discounts offered in the past to any clients that I deal with, so that we can ensure I'm in the best position to make the most suitable quotes in the future. This same process would also be helpful for the other sales reps who have started recently and future newcomers."

Reassurance: Then it's time for your reassuring headline message. This could be "I'm really keen to do everything I can to make sales flow smoothly and to help our business keep existing customers as happy as possible. I was thinking you might like to consider changing the system for sales reps so that we share all information about discounts – and so that it's easy to see through our intranet which clients have been offered what discounts in the past."

Example: In order to bring this headline message alive, you could come down the "Ladder of Abstraction" and show how this sharing of information has worked elsewhere.

"For example, at my last company we introduced a system to share information about discounts offered to all clients and it meant that

new sales reps were able to hit their targets more easily and the quotes offered were always consistent with what had been offered before."

How the care approach helps

So what is this kind of answer likely to achieve?

1. It has maximized the chances of calming the Sales Director by touching his emotions at the outset, recognizing the pressure that's been put on him.

2. It allows you to avoid being stuck on the back foot about who was to blame. This approach could even prompt an apology to you, which would be appropriate and would be a welcome bonus.

3. It has focused the conversation on solving the client's pain and making the Sales Director and Managing Director happier by looking at the possibility of revising the quote.

4. It has suggested a way of helping ensure that you and other newcomers avoid running into the same problem with other clients. So, it puts you in the position of being seen to help yourself and others get better outcomes for Company A and its clients.

5. It conveys a positive, reassuring message about your keenness to do your new job successfully in a way that is in everybody's interests.

Admittedly it could be considered by some to be your line manager's job to put forward positive changes to improve the process. But wherever you are in the hierarchy, there is something to be said for "managing upwards" when required, by helping those above you to make positive changes for the benefit of yourself and others.

By ending the answer on a positive example, it could lead to the next question to you being about exactly how the discount-sharing system worked successfully at another company. This potentially puts the conversation on a far more positive pathway.

Overall, this approach would prevent you from buying into a dangerous false premise (i.e., that the situation was your fault). From the outset your answer puts you in a position to steer the conversation away from a negative, emotionally charged situation and place it on a positive, solution-orientated trajectory – and one that is potentially in the best interests of your company, the client, the relationship between you and your questioner and your fellow sales reps.

Switching formula as you need to

Utilizing the CARE formula in your first answer in a fraught situation gives you the prospect of putting your questioners in a more amenable emotional state.

After you have connected with their hearts, you are better placed to guide the conversation towards more constructive outcomes.

Once the initial emotional element has been acknowledged, you can revert back to the ABCDE formula as challenging fact-based questions arise.

However, always come back to the CARE formula if you are asked further emotionally charged questions.

By using the appropriate formula at each stage of the conversation, you can answer questions when something has gone seriously wrong in a way that best appeals to both your audience's heart and head – and puts you and your questioners in a better place.

Chapter 7

MAXIMIZING THE IMPACT OF YOUR EXAMPLES AND STORIES

You will have noticed that both golden formulae for answering tough questions end on the same letter – "E" for example – which in some cases means a true story. Examples and stories enable you to conclude your answers on a picture that you project into listeners' minds. If they have a positive ending this makes it far more likely that the next question will be more sympathetic. When you select the right example/story for the right audience, the follow-up question may even be: "Can you do the same thing for me with the same fantastic result?" And that of course doesn't qualify as a tough question at all!

This chapter focuses on how to structure your stories and examples to squeeze the maximum amount of juice from everything in that treasure chest you're hopefully starting on your computer or in a box on your desk. Getting the structure right helps put you in the best possible place when it comes to illustrating the messages you're seeking to convey in your answers, to get you off the back foot and decisively onto the front foot.

Story telling is a learnable skill

Some people seem to be natural story tellers. They appear to have an instinctive feel for grabbing attention, gripping an audience throughout and getting exactly the reaction they want at the end. However, if you look closely, you'll notice they often follow a pattern in the way they structure what they say – which they've either learned or worked out for themselves.

And of course there are the opposites – those people who don't seem to have this tale-telling ability at all. They get bogged down in all sorts of potholes along the way – or won't even try. The good news is that telling effective stories is a learnable skill, as someone we shall call Brad could tell you.

Brad is a successful businessman in his mid-sixties. He was among a group of chief executives who gathered from across south-west England to take part in one of my half-day communications-boosting sessions. Members of the group arrived for an early breakfast at a plush hotel in the centre of the old port city of Bristol, in anticipation of supercharging their answering skills. They had, as requested, courageously sent in their toughest questions in advance.

Chief executives know all too well that the hardest questions in a company tend to flow upwards to the top, so they readily recognize their need for such a session. Despite their business experience, they often struggle with the nightmare questions that come from their prospects, their customers, their would-be financiers and their own staff.

They need to answer to questions like: "Are you going to personally take a pay cut because company profits have slipped?" "Isn't it time you retired and let one of our talented young executives take the firm to new heights?" "Why should anyone buy from your company given the recent problems you've had hitting delivery targets?"

As business leaders grapple with such questions, there can be spectacular crashes. Brad was one who was prone to crash. However, he and his fellow chief executives had an enticing incentive to avoid such crashes as the day went on. At the start of the session they learned that the biggest improver during the morning would not just get glory and accolades from their colleagues. They would also win "The Prize" – in this case a glossily packaged triple-CD set of communications tips that I had produced with the legendary South African sales and marketing guru Frank Furness. I'd been advised by a prominent psychologist that if I stroked "The Prize" affectionately, the thought of winning it would seem even more desirable. I stroked "The Prize" a lot that morning. But I hardly needed to. Chief executives are a competitive breed. They like to win. Most of all they want to avoid one of the worst things in the world for them – the ignominy of performing badly in front of their equals.

To measure the amount participants improve, there's a scoring system where everyone is given a mark out of ten by the person beside them based on the quality of their first answer. It's a secret score – never to be revealed under any circumstances. This helps ensure that judging is ruthlessly honest. Then – after they've had the kind of guidance you're receiving in this book and after doing a series of practice exercises – participants have a second go at the same questions. Again this is marked secretly out of ten. In a climactic moment towards the end of the session, the difference between the first and second scores is revealed. The participant who makes the biggest leap between their initial and final attempt is awarded "The Prize".

Brad was an enthusiastic talker, but he was nonetheless the one who floundered most with his first attempt to answer his question.

He'd established a business that everyone present agreed ran impressive operations to help people in practical ways in under-developed countries. Brad knew every aspect of the business thoroughly. His problem was that he didn't know when or how to stop talking about it. As a result, his replies would lead him into verbal traps as he thrashed around searching for an endpoint. His answers became increasingly hesitant and unconvincing as they continued, sometimes stumbling and eventually fizzling out like a firework in a storm. The ultimate cause of Brad's rambling answers was that when he started his replies, he had no idea where they would lead or how they would conclude. It's a common syndrome if you listen for it.

We worked on getting Brad to plan his answers as if telling a joke. It wasn't a matter of being funny of course, but one admirable thing about a well-told joke is that the teller knows at the outset exactly where and how it will end. They can therefore wrap it up decisively with just the right line to get the right result. We worked on Brad's "joke-like" structure. Instead of a punchline, he ended on a gritty example of how his company was helping the poorest people in one of the world's poorest countries. During several rehearsals we worked out exactly the words he would use to bring his example to a close. With practice and encouragement from colleagues around the table, Brad's answers became smoother, crisper and more absorbing, with his conclusion told in a more disciplined and decisive way.

But we couldn't be sure if Brad would get it right when it came to the big test-out moment towards the end of the session. When it came to the climactic official last round of question answering – the one that would determine everyone's overall improvement score – Brad was under pressure. The room was tense. Even the others competing for the biggest improvement wanted him to succeed. Brad faltered a couple of times in his delivery. But each time he recovered quickly and got back on track – avoiding earlier crashes. He came to the final example. And he ended it definitively on the planned final line. Then he stopped. Brad had nailed it! There was applause and relief.

The businesswoman who was scoring Brad determined that the difference from his first to his last performance was a massive eight points out of ten. You can work out from that that his first secret score must have been pretty low and the second secret score pretty high. This improvement jump was a record. Brad won "The Prize".

Shape your example to give that great finish

The challenge facing those like Brad is knowing how best to structure answers – especially that vital closing part when you get to conclude with your example or story. Getting it right rounds off your answer in a satisfying way, so that your story or example sounds exactly as if your reply has come to its natural end. It parcels up your answer like a ribbon around a present.

Here are my guidelines to maximize the effectiveness of your stories and examples.

1. **Think about the outcome you want your example/story to achieve.** When you're planning how to reply to a particular tough question, start with the end in mind by focusing on: "What do I want my audience thinking or feeling or doing when I finish?"

   Do you want your questioner to go "Aha!", "Aaawww", "Oh no!", "Wow", "I want to buy one of those" – or something else?

2. **Choose a relevant example or story in advance.** Dip into your ever-expanding treasure chest of examples and stories and select the most relevant one to achieve the right effect. It's vital to choose your example or story in advance where possible. If you pick it on the run while answering questions it's easy to select one that doesn't quite work and that doesn't achieve exactly the outcome you seek.

3. **Shape the story to make it work for the message you want to convey.** When you have selected the right piece of treasure from your chest you need to focus on the right aspects to shape it in the way that makes it work for the message you're seeking to illustrate.

   Of course, you need to tell exact truths and include enough facts to underline credibility. You also have to allow for the complexity of truth. But this doesn't mean you have to exhaustively say everything about it, which was part of Brad's problem. With story telling you have to be selective. There may be times when giving just a few details of a particular example or case study paints the picture you want in the audience's mind.

4. **To simplify the task, break your story into a start, middle and end.**

   Start: Typically, a great story will have a beginning that sets the scene by giving some evocative details to bring it alive. You introduce the main character. If this character is you, then identify your role within the story. A bit of self-deprecation is often endearing at this point, as audiences warm to a burst of modesty. The start often outlines any challenge involved. At this stage you can project ahead and give listeners something to worry about – such as an especially difficult aspect of the challenge. You can also give them something to look forward to, such as a happy vision of what success would look like.

Middle: This is where most of the action happens. Good things occur. Bad things occur. Some suspense is desirable to keep the audience riveted. A slice of dialogue can help your story shine out: "I said to the client: 'My proposed solution could trigger uncontrollable outrage when your team first hears about it. Some could even quit.' He replied: 'Let's go with it anyway.'"

End: Here your story typically reaches a climax and some kind of resolution. It may be a happy finish – often the case when your company overcomes a challenge and solves a client's problem. But it could be a tragic ending. If you're fundraising for a charity and you include in your answer a story about a victim of the problem the charity seeks to overcome, it may be more effective to finish your answer with a tear-jerkingly unhappy ending – the kind of outcome your charity is seeking to eliminate in future, with the help of enough donations.

Preparing stories that stick

Whether you go for a story with a positive or a negative conclusion, if you have picked the right piece of treasure and presented it in the right way it should leave your audience thinking, feeling or doing what you set out to achieve. People who give great answers end up effectively directing the thoughts and emotions of their listeners with their well-selected and well-delivered examples and stories. Like that punchline in a joke, you need to have the last line well planned out to make your story or example end with oomph.

Here's a story I've designed to highlight this start–middle–end format. It's to illustrate a message about how determined and daring you may have to be if you set out on an ambitious environmental protection mission. The story aims to grab your attention at the beginning, keep you glued during the middle, and channel your emotions in a certain way at the end. I've used fiction here to illustrate the points – but you should only do that in a real answer if you tell your audience it's fiction. This story may be more dramatic, and rather longer, than the one you put in the final part of your answer. But it's designed to stick in your mind, to help you remember the structure.

Set the scene at the start

It's a hot, steamy day in the centre of the biggest city in South America, São Paulo, where massive crowds have gathered to watch one of the most daring human stunts ever attempted. A rope has been strung between the tops of two skyscrapers where Luiz – a devilishly handsome moustachioed circus tightrope walker wearing a big black top hat – plans to walk across the chasm between the two buildings and then walk back to his lofty starting point. If Luiz succeeds, the stunt will raise US$10 million for a charity working to save endangered animals of the Brazilian rainforest – including jaguars and the pink Amazon River dolphin.

Inspired by a similar feat in Chicago, where the tightrope hero wore a blindfold on his return walk, Luiz has decided to wear a blindfold in both directions. And to enhance the atmosphere and draw attention to Brazilian wildlife, the sponsors have set up a large temporary swimming pool in the street below the massive drop. It's been filled with sharp-toothed flesh-eating piranha from the Amazon, which will be returned to their native habitat after the stunt.

Luiz's vivacious girlfriend Gabriela is on top of one building helping him prepare. Gabriela is a circus knife thrower. To add to the drama – and the amount of money collected from sponsors – on Luiz's way back (if he gets that far), Gabriela plans to throw a knife through the air, aiming to knock Luiz's hat off. This is scheduled for the half-way point on the rope immediately above the piranha pool. If she succeeds in doing this without drawing blood, the sponsors have agreed to pay double the amount they've pledged. This would take the total for the rainforest animal charity to US$20 million.

The middle – where most action happens

The crowd roars from the tops of surrounding buildings and the streets below as Luiz, carrying a long balancing pole, makes a confident start with his first few steps onto the rope. Then he suddenly trips. Everyone watching collectively gasps and goes eerily quiet. Luiz's on one leg struggling to remain upright. With the help of the balancing pole he steadies himself and gets both feet back on the rope. A close-up of his face on the live television coverage shows sweat trickling down one cheek. Another shot shows Gabriella with her hands over her face, peeking through her fingers.

Luiz continues. He gets to the point immediately over the piranha pool. Then he slips again. This time it's worse. He's quivering on one leg. But he struggles to get back on balance. He moves on, looking remarkably composed. Then he gets to the last bit of the rope that slopes upwards slightly as it reaches the second building. Luiz slows and concentrates hard. His last few steps up the last part of the rope are awkward. But he gets there and is hugged crazily by his support team. The crowd goes wild. Then Luiz turns around to go back.

Just as he's about to take his first step, Gabriella takes her hands away from her face and screams out across the chasm from the other building: "Don't do it, Luiz. It's not worth it. I love you too much!" Luiz takes one hand off the balancing pole and waves in her direction. He smiles reassuringly, then steps onto the rope. A quarter of the way along the rope he stops. A wind has sprung up. The flags on top of nearby buildings start to flutter. Luiz remains motionless on the rope. The crowd is hushed. Then the flags go limp. Luiz waits a few seconds. He continues. He edges closer to the middle. Then he stops and waits, immediately over the piranha pool. For the first time, his head tilts down. But of course the blindfold means he can't see a thing.

Gabriella picks up the knife. She wets the middle finger on her right hand to test for the breeze. The flags are flapping a little. She pulls her left hand back and hurls the knife, spinning it through the air. The camera shot from behind her shows it's heading slightly to the side of her target. But it curves in with the breeze. It clips the side of the top hat. The hat topples off. Luiz shakes a bit, then steadies. There's a massive collective sigh of relief from the crowd. The knife plummets. It splashes into the pool. A zoom-in shot of the piranhas shows that they don't noticeably react. The top hat falls more slowly. Getting caught by the breeze, it lands beside the pool. A small girl in a multi-coloured flowery dress breaks away from the crowd on the pavement and collects it. She puts it on her head. It swamps her. She looks ridiculous. People applaud. The girl smiles.

Way, way above Luiz starts walking again – very slowly. He's going at half the pace that he was before. Each step is measured and tentative. About ten steps to go. He's at the bit where the rope begins to slope upwards. Nine steps to go. Eight to go. Then he slips again. It's a worse slip than before. He's actually hopping on the rope. He arches his back to stay in the air. Again Gabriella buries her face in her hands. Luiz's so near to the edge of the building. Is he going to fall at this late stage? He steadies himself. He's back on balance. The close-up shows him looking ashen.

The ending – where you draw the threads together

Seven steps to go. Luiz's on track. Six to go. He speeds his walking. Five steps to go. He's almost bounding along now. Four, three, two, one. He's made it! Luiz is engulfed in Gabriella's arms. The team around him on the building jump wildly. So do the team members on the opposite building. The crowds below and around break into the mightiest of roars. They're so loud you might think the jaguars and even the pink dolphins could hear them.

Later that day, before the world's media, Luiz and Gabriella declare that they will become rangers in the Amazon rainforest, working directly to help protect the animals. Luiz promises Gabriella he will never perform a death-defying feat again.

Applying the rules to your example or story

So, the end of your great answer isn't necessarily going to be quite like the Luiz/Gabriella story – but it can have some of the same dramatic elements. Let's look at how the start–middle–end format can work with the kind of example you might deploy to end an answer to a question about your organization from a potential customer.

The message you are seeking to illustrate will typically be something like:

> *"Our organization is doing remarkable things to help people deal with this kind of challenge."*

Whatever your role in the organization, it's always good to have examples in your treasure chest that highlight the good work it's doing. You can even follow the pattern of an American broom-carrying janitor who was questioned by President John F. Kennedy during his visit to the National Aeronautics and Space Administration (NASA) in 1962. When the janitor was asked what he was doing, he reportedly replied: "Well Mr President, I'm helping put a man on the moon."

However, if your organization's mission is big enough, you can say a bit more than that – and you don't have to make it sound too easy! It's good public relations for you and your organization.

The essence of public relations has been summed up in an impressive but grammatically flawed way as "Doing good and telling people about it."

And on the principle that it's better to show not tell, having a prepared example of something that your organization is beavering away at can be used to round off a range of questions. This can form part of the response to the question that President Kennedy posed.

Funnily enough, a lot of people regard the "What do you do?" question as a really tough one. It shouldn't normally be the case. This is a question that effectively invites you to give what's known as your "elevator pitch". That is what to say to someone you meet briefly in a lift, if they ask you between floors about your role and that of your organization. Having that great example ready is supremely useful to round off your reply. A powerful positive example can also be useful to conclude any of those much harder questions you might get about what your organization is up to.

Let's suppose you are working in the pharmaceuticals sector for Company Z, which is doing something indisputably good – seeking a way to make it easier for smokers to give up their habit and stop being held hostage to the highly addictive drug nicotine.

The outcome you're looking for from an audience of, say, university science students is: "Wow, what a great company. I'd love to work there when I finish my degree."

So your headline message might be: "Company Z is involved in ambitious projects that will benefit humankind."

When it comes to giving an example, you could say something like the following.

Start: "Company Z is seeking to solve some of the most challenging problems involving improving human health. For example, we're trying to make it easier for smokers who want to quit. Our top scientists are concentrating on developing a new product to help smokers, which doesn't involve giving them what's called 'nicotine replacement therapy' and which is better for them."

Middle: "The challenge for us is to come up with a product that doesn't have any of the bad side-effects that nicotine replacement therapy has. People who take that can get things like disturbed sleep, upset stomachs, dizziness and headaches. Formulating a tablet that doesn't cause any of these problems is a difficult challenge. The first tablet we came up with didn't do well in early drug trials. However, we learnt some really useful things from the initial trials and now we have a massive new trial involving hundreds of volunteers and the early results are phenomenally promising."

End: "If our new tablet can be shown to work without serious side-effects then we are confident that as many as half of those who smoke in this country will be able to quit more easily and add many healthy years to their lives. We're then planning to export it everywhere."

An answer like this could well make future scientific geniuses say "Hey, how do I get a job at Company Z?"

Prepare those oven-ready stories

Whichever line of work you're in, it's desirable to have well-structured, oven-ready examples and stories to tell about you and your organization that you can slot in to conclude your answers – to inspire your audiences and help get the outcomes you seek.

Chapter 8

GETTING YOUR PERFORMANCE RIGHT

Think of a time when you glimpsed a television programme in a language you didn't understand. I bet that you quickly formed views about the personalities you saw and heard on screen – whether you liked them, would believe them or trust them.

You couldn't have made those judgments based on what the personalities were actually saying. Rather, your view must have been driven by how they looked and how they sounded.

When conversing with people, we make judgments about them constantly. Of course they're doing the same with us – probably more so when we're answering their questions than at any other time.

You have to conclude that a big part of these judgments is due to what's interpreted from voices, facial expressions and what people do with their bodies.

Experts debate how much each of these particular individual factors counts. Their relative importance can clearly differ from one person to another, and from one situation to another. But there's universal agreement that the actual words uttered form only a part of what's communicated when anyone is speaking.

It's vital to take this into account when considering how we come across while being questioned. It can have a decisive effect on what people think, feel and do as a result of our answers.

It's fair to say that some people naturally know how to project themselves with authority, impact and persuasiveness. But it's also fair to say that this is something you can work at and improve.

This does not mean that there's a fundamental need to change your values, beliefs or personality. It just means learning different ways of projecting the real you and enhancing what you already do.

Watch yourself back and adjust

Video playbacks can help you improve enormously. If you see and hear yourself as others do, you can dramatically refine the way you come across while under cross-examination. If the real you is made even more fantastic in the process, as can happen, then that's a bonus.

So, whenever you get the opportunity to watch and listen to yourself back, grab it. Be warned though, that video playbacks aren't always comfortable viewing. There's a certain "yuk factor", which many experience during the process. Please persist.

If you can cope heroically with this rugged reality check, you can reap amazing benefits! When I run communications-boosting sessions, I like to have a camera operator so everyone gets to experience what their answers are really like. As with eating green vegetables, it may not be tasty. But like broccoli and spinach, it's good for you.

In this chapter we'll look at what aspects of your body language and voice delivery are effectively communicating, and help you adjust to project the ideal image you want.

While that ideal image naturally differs from person to person, there's a remarkable similarity in what people aspire to when it comes to that image of themselves they'd like to convey. When I send out pre-session forms for participants before master classes, I ask them to write the descriptive words they'd like others to choose to define them at their best. Popular choices include "confident", "authentic", "honest", "friendly" and "impressive". I'll assume it's likely that you, too, would want to be seen as all these, among other things. So, the recommendations on body and voice usage here are designed to help you convey these kinds of traits and others you'd like to project.

Project the best version of you

The number one guiding rule in dealing with the way you come across is to be yourself. However, I'm more ambitious for you than that. I want you to be the BEST VERSION of yourself – every time you're answering questions in a professional capacity.

So draw upon the answer to the question posed earlier: "What's at the heart of you?" Whatever that is, it should shine through when you're answering questions. If you're being true to yourself then this will be conveyed through your body, voice and the general aura you project.

How you position your body and how you enable yourself to sound govern not only how you're perceived by others. Crucially, they affect how you feel at the time you're giving your answers. This is critical to the confidence you experience and transmit.

For the purposes of portraying the best possible image of yourself, you should be feeling as splendid as possible when being questioned. When you feel calm, confident and in control, it's so much easier to project these qualities to your audience.

Be a great performer

When answering questions – whether from one person or an audience of thousands – it's important to realize that you're actually performing. This is different from – and not to be confused with – acting. Your performance should be totally genuine. But recognize and accept that you're on display and being judged. If that feels daunting, just run with the idea of performing for the moment – and hopefully you'll warm to the concept!

We'll now cover a range of ways that your performance is vital to how you and your answers are perceived. The starting point is what you should be doing with your body overall.[1]

We'll examine what to do when you're sitting, but first let's look at when you're standing to answer questions.

Stand tall with your feet on the ground

While standing, keep both soles firmly planted on the ground – typically shoulder-width apart – or place one foot slightly more forward than the other. Keep your weight spread evenly on both feet. This makes you look and feel properly secure and literally "grounded".

When feeling nervous, some people stand on one leg and bend the other, often crossing at the ankles. This means that one leg takes a disproportionate amount of your weight. It sends a message to your

---

[1]   Note that this is largely directed at enhancing performance in professional conversations in the western world. If you are answering questions elsewhere, there is much to be said for getting guidance on the cultural norms relating to performance in the place you are going to. You can then apply – and adjust – what is recommended in this chapter with that in mind.

GETTING YOUR PERFORMANCE RIGHT

brain that you're feeling unbalanced. In contrast, with two feet firmly anchored you look and feel much more stable and confident.

Without wishing to sound like a nagging head teacher, stand erect. However short or tall you are, allow yourself to stretch up to your full height. Tall people – especially tall women, I find – can tend to stoop in an apologetic way when conscious that they're towering above others. Ultimately it looks best to be all of who you are. Drawing yourself fully upright is ideal for ensuring you look your best to others – and, crucially, feel your best about yourself.

There's an approach I like to call "string theory", where you pretend you're a puppet on strings. Imagine that one string runs up your backbone and continues, where it connects with your head and protrudes though the top of your skull. Before stepping into the spotlight you metaphorically tug upwards at the top of the string above your head to ensure you're standing at your full height. By being completely upright you look more authoritative and composed to your questioners.[2]

Move with a purpose

In a typical one-to-one professional conversation it's generally best that you remain in one spot. If you're on stage or in some kind of forum answering questions from an audience, then it's appropriate to move around at certain times. But there's a supremely important rule governing this: when you move, do so with a purpose. Wandering up and down like a caged animal is

---

[2] This technique was passed on to me by the actor Neil Roberts, when he was working with the training company Partners With You.

distracting – and invites your audience to focus less on what you're saying and more on the pattern you're tracing.

Moving with a purpose helps build rapport and understanding. Shift position to ensure you're facing the questioner in an audience. Head towards the front of the stage if you have something intimate to share with the gathering. Move towards the back of the stage if you want to project a grand vision or a helicopter view.

It can be good to move around to effectively re-enact things when you get to the story part of an answer. For example, if you're talking about something that happened when you were strolling between one place and another, it aids communication to do a planned walk across the stage as you do it.

Liberate your arms

Where you put your arms when answering questions is vital to how you're perceived. You come across as more engaging when your arms are actively involved.

I encourage answerers to deliver what I call the "Full Body Experience". The premise is that when dealing with the question, you want to be giving the audience your all. When you put your whole body into dealing with their question then it comes across as completely sincere. You're physically demonstrating that you're putting everything into dealing with their question.

Giving the "Full Body Experience" largely comes down to what you do with your arms. When you're answering – as opposed to listening to – the question, have your arms up and hold them apart with your hands open. By doing this you're physically demonstrating to your questioner that you are open to connect with them.

Having your arms up and open sometimes feels awkward at the start of your answer. But it looks right. First impressions count massively, so it enables you to look engaging from the outset. When you begin like this you can feel more at ease with it quickly. You'll probably find that your arms and hands automatically start involving themselves and physically reinforcing what you're saying in a most helpful way. Without thinking about it, you may start doing things like counting on your fingers as you make numbered points. This aids audience understanding of what you're saying.

When planning the story/example component of an answer, it's good to work out specific gestures for particular points. But be aware that once your hands get into play they tend to take on a life of their own. Providing you remain conscious of what your hands are doing – and ensure they avoid being too annoyingly distracting – this should be a good thing too.

Beware what body language experts call "tells" – signs given off unthinkingly from your body that indicate you may not be as comfortable as you'd like to be. Tells can "leak out" what's really going on in your head. For example, jerky or "windmilling" arm movements suggest agitation. To project confidence, you want your arms and hands to be controlled. Smooth movements generally impress.

Having your hands up and open prevents them doing a number of things that send the wrong signal. As far as humanly possible, avoid touching yourself while answering. Steer clear of having your hands in contact with your face in particular, as this can be interpreted as covering up and being less than truthful. Scratching or rubbing yourself anywhere can make you look unsettled.

Because first impressions last, it's ideal to have your arms involved from the beginning. Avoid starting with your arms rigid and then "warming up" in front of your audience. You ought to come across as totally warmed up at the start, in the same way that dancers and actors do at the beginning of a show. They make a point of doing warm-up exercises before performing – enabling them to be in top performance mode the moment the curtains are raised. It's commendable for question answerers too to be physically warmed up before the conversation starts. Try a bit of discreet behind-the-scenes stretching or light exercise before the big occasion.

If you feel excessively self-conscious, having your arms apart when you start talking, one option is to have a (normally non-alcoholic) drink in one hand. By giving one hand something practical to do, it can make you feel more comfortable to have your arms apart. As the conversation progresses you normally become increasingly relaxed, so having your arms apart can feel more natural. You can put the drink down and carry on answering with your hands apart when you feel comfortable.

Study those weather forecasters

Television weather forecasters tend to be excellent models of friendly, open body language. As they interpret their maps, the forecasters you see on western television typically have their arms flowing openly and smoothly. This projects a comfortable, fully involved approach for viewers. Their arms usually move gracefully whatever the weather – even when warning of destructive hurricanes. This smooth involvement of their arms can have a reassuring effect. The weather may be out of control but from the warmth of their studio, they are in control.

If you're an arm-moving sceptic – and there are a few out there – consider the opposite of involving your arms in your professional conversations. This can result in you looking static and even awkward. I hope this encourages you to metaphorically embrace your audience with your arms (without actually touching anyone!) and avoid the "non-engagement arm positions" outlined here.

Five common non-engagement arm positions to avoid

1. **Don't have your arms permanently by your sides.** I call this the "Firing Squad Position", because it looks as though the straight-down-arms person being questioned thinks they're about to be shot. They tend to look wooden, uncomfortable and even scared.

2. **Keep clear of the "Free Kick Defensive Wall" position.** During a free kick in football (soccer), defenders bunch together to block the kicker's line of sight to the goal. They routinely clasp their hands in front of their groins. This protects them from being hurt in a particularly painful spot if the ball is kicked straight at them. It makes pain-avoiding sense. But it also makes the players look and feel defensive. Similarly, if you stand with your hands covering your groin when answering questions, you will look and feel equally defensive.

3. **Don't clasp your arms behind your back in what the military call "standing at ease".** Far from allowing you to come across "with ease", this can signal that you're not willing to fully engage. Senior male members of the British royal family often adopt this position when on walkabout to meet the "commoners". It can give the impression: "I'm here because I have to be and I don't want to fully connect with you." This interpretation may be unfair, but appearances matter. In

contrast, having your arms and hands up and open looks and feels as though you're making a wholehearted effort to engage with those around you.

4. **Refrain from folding your arms across your chest.** This can look uncaring and excessively defensive – with even a menacing hint of aggression. As with other aspects of body language interpretation, there can be incorrect readings of this. It could be that an answerer with arms folded just happens to feel more comfortable that way – or that they're cold. But if you reply with folded arms, you don't normally appear enthusiastic about what you're saying.

5. **Finally, keep your hands out of your pockets while answering.** Quite simply, without your hands on display you don't look fully involved. Be aware, if you're male, that women overwhelmingly don't like to see you with your hands in your pockets – especially if it involves rattling loose change!

How to project when sitting

Positioning yourself properly when seated is most important. There's an easy-to-remember rule – encapsulated in the letters "BBC". This stands for putting your Bottom at the Back of the Chair. Perching on the edge of your seat can make you look nervous and unsettled. Lounging back too far in a chair suggests complacency.

- **Don't slump or slouch.** You want to be fairly upright from the waist up. While remaining straight-backed, tilt ever so slightly in the direction of your questioner/s. This physically demonstrates that you're keen to give answers.
- **Avoid crossing your legs above the knee.** This can look defensive, as if the upper leg is shielding you from attack. It can

also prevent you from getting the full quota of air in your lungs, needed for projecting your voice.

- **Keep both feet planted on the floor – if they will reach – to give that "grounded" look and feel.** Those wearing a dress or skirt can come across in a more "ladylike" way by keeping their legs parallel to each other rather than crossing them.
- **The "arms and hands open" rule still applies when sitting.** If you're at a desk or table, have your arms apart and resting on the surface. Raise your arms above the desk when making important points. Avoid the temptation to clasp your hands tightly together in front of you, as this looks defensive. As a general rule, banging your fist on the desk or slapping the table comes across as shockingly aggressive.

Get it right with your face

The part of you that your listeners will normally focus on is your face. This is one reason why their view of it shouldn't be blocked by hands.

My key rule for facial expressions is that they should be in harmony with the content of what you're saying at every point. Your face will (mostly) automatically take care of this without much concentration. But if your facial expression gets out of line with what you're saying, it can be jarring for your audience.

Let's contemplate an answer you give using the CARE formula if something bad has happened involving distress for your questioner. When expressing your concern at the start of the answer, you must look suitably serious. An accidental smile when talking about someone's tragic death looks awful (yes, it can happen in a totally unintended and unmeant way).

Smile when appropriate. In a typical ABCDE-type answer, where you move to a positive example at the end, look appropriately happy as you reveal the wondrous details.

Where your eyes look is critical

- **Maintain eye contact with your questioner/s as much as possible.** This signals that you're focused on them and that they're important to you. You can also observe the reactions you're getting and adjust your delivery style as appropriate.
- **Be careful not to let it turn into a staring competition.** In a one-to-one conversation, you can look directly into your questioner's eyes much of the time. But ensure this doesn't turn into an intimidating stare. If you sense that your questioner feels uncomfortable, then look more generally at their face.
- **Breaking eye contact in the wrong way sends a negative message.** Looking upwards to the heavens appears as if you're seeking advice from the powers above because you don't know the answer. Looking downwards can make you appear guilty or ashamed. Moving your head or eyes from side to side gives the impression that you don't know where the correct answer can be found.
- **Share your eye contact when you have an audience.** Allow your eyes to roam slowly around various parts of an audience – whether large or small. With a big crowd you can keep your gaze largely directed just above the heads in the back row, which gives the impression that you're focused on everyone.
- **The exception to the eye contact rule.** There's one time in particular in a one-to-one conversation when it's acceptable to break eye contact. It's just before you start a particularly thoughtful answer or a deeply personal one. Breaking off eye contact here allows you to move momentarily into your own "private space" to contemplate your response. Done correctly,

this looks respectful to your questioner as it gives the impression of maximum thought being employed to construct an accurate answer. However, don't go into your private space too often as this can potentially look evasive. And when doing television interviews never go visually into your private space, as it can (unfairly) make you look less than straightforward to your viewing audience.

- **Avoid excessive blinking.** This can look as though you're struggling under pressure.

Be careful when listening

Listening to questions is part of your performance. Your arms need to be deployed in a different way while listening, because standing with your arms apart at this time can look odd. I've studied this situation intensely and here is my well-tested advice: when you're in listening mode, it's fine to bring your hands together across your chest. Having your fingertips loosely touching the fingertips on your other hand, as if forming a church steeple a bit below your chin, is acceptable. This allows you to look appropriately thoughtful while absorbing the question. Just make sure you open your arms and hands exactly at the time you open your mouth to begin your answer.

Be aware of the importance of being in control of your face while listening to the question. This is a time to maintain eye contact with the questioner – out of politeness and also to pick up any non-verbal cues to help you more deeply understand their inquiry.

While listening, it's usually best to keep your head and face in neutral mode. Wait until the question is finished before giving an indication of agreement or disagreement to any proposition put forward. Never allow your head to nod up and down while taking in a question, as this implies agreement. If you want to test the wisdom of this in practice, get someone to ask you: "Are you a mad, dangerous criminal out to get people?" and nod your head up and down while listening!

It's wiser to remain poker-faced until the question concludes and then to give yourself a couple of seconds of neutral-looking thinking time before giving your considered answer with the usual full expression.

Use but minimize notes – where necessary

For important occasions, when you're being questioned in front of a potentially tough audience, you may feel that you need a physical reminder of what to say.

It's better to have some notes rather than leave yourself fearing an embarrassingly blank mind on key questions. If you need notes, keep them as brief and unobtrusive as possible. Rather than writing lots of whole sentences, have just a few words – or even a series of single words or symbols – to remind you of the key points. The sparser your notes, the more useful they can be when you're under pressure. This is because, if you look down to see an ocean of words, it's hard to find the right place to prompt the right answer. If you have just a few succinct points, it's so much easier to quickly identify the correct spot and then look up and continue.

Select a tiny piece of paper – or better still cardboard, as it doesn't flap or get scrunched. Something the size of a business card or smaller is good, as it can fit unobtrusively in your palm or be placed discretely on a lectern or desk.

If you're being questioned on a matter involving a large document – such as an annual report or building plan – then it's sensible to have it to hand. Mark key parts in advance so you know where to look at the right moments.

Remember, the last thing you want to be is a prisoner of your notes, who can't give answers without them. But all humans can go blank on the odd fact or figure, so having a tiny prompt or a carefully marked document to glance at during such moments is a reasonable precaution. And in a situation where you are relying on notes, look up from them as often as possible to make eye contact with your questioners.

Rehearse, relax and succeed

When reading about body language it's easy to become overly self-conscious. The trick is to be aware what your body is doing and make adjustments where appropriate without being too focused on it. When you're in the spotlight, you naturally want your primary concentration to be on your content and messages.

If you can get yourself in a relaxed but highly focused state, then the correct body language elements often fall into place. Having well-structured, pre-planned potential answers with excellent content makes it easier to perform and convey your mastery of your subject.

There are several things you can do to ensure you get yourself in the right frame of mind.

First, is to do some rehearsing. When you've planned how to respond to key questions, then practice your potential answers in front of a mirror. In this way you can keep an eye on your body language and tweak your content, structure and delivery style in the privacy of your bedroom. For a really big occasion it's also worth practicing with a colleague or friend asking you questions. The repetition of key lines, phrases and stories develops the neural pathways in your brain. When you can comfortably recall what you plan to say, it's much easier to focus on *how* you come across.

You don't need to practice to the point of being word perfect – because in the robustness of a challenging conversation you will always be adapting what you prepared to fit the context of the moment. But when you can, it's comforting to have key pre-prepared components, which are especially well rehearsed, such as your stories and examples.

Wisdom from a vocal master

Whatever the timbre of your voice and any accent you may have, sounding dramatically more impressive is surprisingly achievable. I know because I discovered this at the feet of a master.

Arch McKirdy was a shining Australian radio star from the 1950s to the 1970s. He presented what became the most popular radio show in the country – *Relax With Me*. When he eventually bade farewell to his show, Arch was made Director of Radio Presentation at the Australian Broadcasting Corporation, where he showed others how to use their voices in order to sound more captivating, more natural and more in control – just as he did.

I was privileged to spend many hours with Arch in one-to-one and group sessions. He had techniques for showing how to deploy words by saying them in a way that was both more entrancing and more meaningful. This was invaluable for bringing sentences to life especially when I was interviewed as an on-the-scene reporter.

Alas Arch is no longer physically with us, but his insights live on. I utilize his techniques repeatedly in my question-answering master classes because they're so effective to help participants' answers sparkle. What follows largely involves chunks of Arch's wisdom, which will hopefully help take you towards sounding as impressive as he did.

Talk warmly – as if to a friend

Arch McKirdy made the point that you should practice your voice-delivery technique when preparing for a large audience by imagining you are talking to one friend. It's so much less daunting to envisage conversing with a single familiar person, rather than lots you don't know.

So, when practicing, picture a friend and say your words as warmly as possible. Aim to deliver the planned words in meaningful groups rather than as individual words. Focus hard on the meaning itself, to make sure that your pictured friend is then able to draw every possible ounce of meaning from those words.

Take that big breath

When you're about to answer a question take a big, slow breath. Draw the air in from down deep – from your diaphragm – not shallowly from your head. To practice this, put your hand on your belly button and make sure this is where you instigate the breath.

The big, slow breath from down low makes you feel instantly refreshed. It's an exhilarating way to go into your great answer with a positive mindset.

Taking the big breath at a leisurely pace avoids sending an adrenalin rush through your body, which can happen if you breathe too quickly. At its most extreme, a burst of adrenalin from someone in a fearful state can reduce the flow of oxygen to their brain and edge them towards saying something unthinkingly stupid.

Starting your answer with your lungs full of air means you can progress a long way through your reply without needing to gasp for additional air. Excessive breathiness can signal that you're under pressure. Having lots of air in your lungs from the start helps you sound well controlled and, where necessary, reassuring.

After your initial big breath, deliver the words while breathing and pausing naturally – just as you do normally, when you breathe at the right times without consciously thinking about it. At the same time, focus your brain not just on what you're telling your audience, but also why.

Go slow to maximize impact

Speaking more slowly than your normal pace helps you underline the significance of your content – and ensures that your listeners have time to absorb the meaning properly. Slowing it down gives more time to get your expression right, as well as your actual content. Listen in news reports to how slowly the highly persuasive Barack Obama or Bill Clinton speak when they have a really important point to make. By speaking slowly they make their points seem more profound.

Take a bath in your answer

Arch McKirdy had a particularly memorable expression – "take a bath" in what you're planning to say. Relax in the midst of your slow and naturally delivered content, so you and your listeners can actually enjoy taking it in.

This also enables you to squeeze maximum meaning and effect out of your words. If you're describing a new "squelchy, squishy" skin cream to spread lovingly and improve skin tone, then allow yourself to bask in the sounds of "squelchy" and "squishy" to ensure the feel of this moistly sensuous product is conveyed with maximum effectiveness.

Emphasize those qualifiers

Arch had a particularly effective technique for getting the emphasis right in every part of a sentence. The secret is to put any emphasis on what he called the "qualifiers". These are the describing words – those adjectives and adverbs. So, if you're talking about *red* apples, *green* apples and *yellow* apples, it sounds so much better for you to emphasize the qualifier rather than the noun – "apples" – that you're describing.

Surprisingly, this emphasis is not typically achieved by saying the describing words louder. Rather, it's a matter of saying them slightly slower and with a different tone of voice – making it clear to your listeners exactly what you mean.

While every element of each sentence is important, the biggest key to sounding impressive is to get the right pitch at the *end* of each sentence. Beware the danger of letting your voice drift upwards at the end of a sentence, making you sound uncertain and insecure. This has been labelled the "Australian upward inflection syndrome" – a most unfortunate Aussie export for which, on behalf of my country, I apologize to the world. Your answers will sound so much more sophisticated and confident when you avoid it. Arch McKirdy drummed it out of his students. I seek to do the same. When you ensure your voice goes down at the end of each sentence, it makes you sound so much more authoritative, in control and profound.

Visualize your success

To get yourself into the right, confident mindset before and while answering questions, visualize your success in advance – by focusing on how you would like to look, sound and feel in that encounter. Picturing the ideal image of yourself in action helps make it a reality. You can do this while rehearsing. You can also do it while walking, swimming or lying down – by allowing yourself to imagine how successfully you will come across in those key moments in the spotlight.

There are uplifting advantages to visualizing and practicing to ensure you get your performance right. This will help you look, sound and feel great. And if you feel great, then it is so much easier to get your audience feeling the same way.

If you get your preparation, rehearsing and visualization right, then you're on track to get your performance right. When you nail that, then even a foreigner who hears and sees you but doesn't speak your language will still be impressed because of the way you shine.

Chapter 9

CONVEYING YOUR ANSWERS TO DIFFERENT PERSONALITY TYPES

Let yourself imagine you're working for an ambitious new international charity. It has put together a bold proposal to ensure everyone on the planet will in future have access to clean drinking water. The proposition needs high-level support in order to become reality. The heads of the charity have targeted four influential world figures who are, or were once, in powerful positions. The hope is to persuade them to personally endorse the plan. But in seeking to get the leaders and former leaders on board, you can expect loads of tough questions from each of them.

The charity has sent the four big names exactly the same written information. The case mounted has been strong enough to persuade each of the four to allow a delegation to visit them in their home country, so they can find out more. You've been selected to take charge of preparations to answer their questions.

As you gather information to become more familiar with the background and styles of the world figures, you're reminded that each of the four have contrasting personalities and ways of behaving. And they will each prefer to have their questions answered in different ways. Your team needs to be ready for this in order to maximize the charity's prospects of success.

The first meeting will be in Moscow with the tough-guy Russian, Vladimir Putin, who likes baring his muscles with his shirt off while riding horses in the rugged Russian wilderness. You look up his history and conclude that Mr Putin is quick to make decisions, such as ordering the use of force to counter developments he sees as being against his interests or those of Russia. You're reminded that he instantly favoured using the powers of the state against the gutsy Russian feminist punk rock protest group, Pussy Riot. Whatever you personally think of Vladimir Putin, you don't want to mess around with someone who acts decisively and isn't excessively patient. You will have to get delegation members ready to deal rapidly with his questions.

You then have to cross the Atlantic and be prepared for potentially highly detailed questions in California from technical whizz Bill Gates, who built the largest personal computer software company on the globe. Your research reminds you that his mastery of detail enabled him to become the world's richest man – and one of its most generous philanthropists. You discover that young Bill was supposedly so knowledgeable at school that he was allowed to skip some mathematics classes because he already knew so much. And you note that despite his wealth and fame, Bill Gates always likes to be on top of the detail of technical things. Even when he stepped down as Chief Executive Officer of Microsoft, he created for himself the position of "Chief Software Architect". You have to ensure that your delegation can satisfy the need Bill Gates could have for answers on issues that might be too technical for the other target names to bother with.

Next you need to fly coast-to-coast back across America for the excitement of a New York meeting in Harlem with the charismatic saxophone-playing Bill Clinton, the former United States President who likes discussing big policy issues in fast-food restaurants among other places. You read that while seeking the presidency –

and when in office – Mr Clinton gained a reputation for (among other things) running behind schedule because he loves exchanging stories with people so much along the way. You will need to have some uplifting stories ready about how smaller projects that have brought clean drinking water to remote and impoverished places have changed lives and brought smiles.

Finally, you will need draft answers ready for what could perhaps be a more quietly thoughtful meeting in London with John Major, the one-time British Prime Minister who, despite his prominence, is hard for some to remember due to his mild-mannered personal style – gracious and charming though he can be face-to-face. When you read up on his period in power, you're reminded that he rose to the top rung in politics in the aftermath of the dominant figure of Margaret Thatcher and in office seemed to remain in her shadow much of the time. You're reminded how John Major spent much of his prime ministership struggling to keep the many disgruntled people around him content – such as members of his own party who were at loggerheads over whether Britain should leave the European Union. You also study how he started the process of patiently bringing together the warring terrorist-backed and anti-violence representatives of the volatile, religiously divided political scene in Northern Ireland to eventually co-operate in creating a more peaceful future.

Crafting answers to persuade specific individuals

Many people have an automatic tendency to treat everyone in much the same way when they communicate. But if you contemplate the differing natures of the four figures you're preparing to meet, you will see the strong advantages of answering them in a way that appeals to each individual. The basic information you give will be the same for each, but your way of getting it across and persuading each personality will need to be different.

There are many methods and systems for classifying humans. And if you can determine the kind of personality type you're dealing with, you can increase your chances of persuading them.

A pioneer in this area is the psychologist Tony Alessandra, who has formulated what he calls "The Platinum Rule". This is a variation of "The Golden Rule" that Jesus Christ advocated, where you "Do unto others as you would wish them to do unto you". Dr Alessandra's rule tweaks this, by advising: "Do unto others as THEY would like done unto THEM".

This means, in a question-and-answer situation, presenting the material in a way that the individual personality would like to receive it – in terms of things like the content selected, pace of delivery, amount of detail and relative balance between factual and emotional elements.

Connecting with four different personality types

Tony Alessandra insightfully classifies people into four broad behavioural types and recommends dealing with each of them in different ways. Each of the big four names identified by the fictitious charity mentioned earlier fits into a different category. When you get to recognize these four types – and seek to classify yourself – you will gain an insight into how best to reveal your truths in order to give answers in the way that each of these types prefers.

I first became familiar with Dr Alessandra's methods while preparing to conduct workshops to help public servants convey difficult messages. The course designers cited Dr Alessandra's work and his simple way of classifying people on a continuum ranging from introvert to extrovert and on another continuum ranging from people-orientated to task-orientated.

Dr Alessandra makes the point that his categories are based on observable behavioural patterns. But as you look at the different types, remember that people are of course complex and not always entirely consistent. People who may normally fit into one category can default to a secondary category in some circumstances – within a conversation or when shifting from one environment to another, such as from home to work. And people, being unique, can of course exhibit behaviour from different categories at the same time. But whatever behavioural style best defines you, I expect you'll agree that Dr Alessandra's categories can be profoundly useful when planning and delivering answers in one-to-one meetings. They're also profoundly useful in situations where you're speaking to lots of people from the same personality type together in a room, such as at a convention of football managers, surveyors, cruise-ship entertainers or receptionists.

The following sections set out what Dr Alessandra has classified as the four behavioural styles – and I have supplemented his outlines with some experiences I've had working with examples of people in the categories he defines.

The four types are:

1. **Directors** – characteristic "boss" types, such as Vladimir Putin.

2. **Thinkers** – those who revel in technical details, such as accountants, engineers and computer enthusiasts like Bill Gates.

3. **Socializers** – those who love mixing with lots of people, such as television quiz show hosts and other enthusiastic talkers like Bill Clinton.

4. **Relaters** – those who focus on trying to keep those around them happy, like John Major.

1. THE DIRECTOR – who Tony Alessandra labels "The Great Initiator"

These are extrovert, task-orientated people often found in positions of power. Think Margaret Thatcher. Or picture those hirers-and-firers from the business world on the television show *The Apprentice* – Alan Sugar in the British version and Donald Trump in the American version – who relish grilling contestants and then removing those they see as underperformers.

The most important thing for the Director personality is getting the job done and hitting the right bottom line. This person tends to be direct, competitive and can appear impatient. They don't take long to say: "You're fired!" Directors like to dominate and be in control. They're attracted to specific, measurable results.

Directors will be concerned with the question: "How will this help me and my organization do the job better and faster?" Tony Alessandra makes the point that Directors don't tend to be naturally good listeners. And, putting himself predominantly in this category, he makes a self-deprecating joke, asking: "Why would Directors want to listen when they already know the answer?" Remember this when talking with Vladimir Putin.

Nonetheless, Directors tend to ask a lot of questions, and when they do so they want straight-to-the-point answers. They don't normally relish lots of details, providing enough are given for responses to be credible.

Directors will sometimes vigorously ask a series of questions with the main aim being to test out the credibility of the answerer rather than to seek information for its own sake. For example, I remember being in front of an audience of chief executives – many of whom were, hardly surprisingly, Director types. One peppered me with sceptical inquiries about my recommended approach to handling questions. He showed little enthusiasm for my answers at the time. But a few days afterwards he booked me to work with his two sales teams in northern and southern England to teach them the same methods. I had passed his test. He wasn't concerned about whether his fierce questions might offend me, or even whether he completely understood my methods. Ultimately, he wanted to know if I could help with the kind of thing Director types really care about – his company's sales team performance. He needed his team to deal more effectively with questions from their prospects during sales conversations, which hadn't been going as successfully as he wanted.

I had a similar experience the day I did a professional-speaking audition for Director-type business experts who run peer-learning sessions for groups of company leaders. As part of my session I did a tough demonstration interview with one of them – featuring characteristic "blowtorch-on-the-belly" questions. I then showed how he could come across more impressively by changing the way he structured and delivered his answers. When I had finished the fast-track makeover, one of the experts watching in the audience snarled: "We really liked your stuff. But we didn't like you much. What can you do about that?" I was a touch shocked by the unexpected aggression, and can't recall my exact answer. I do remember using the ABCDE formula, and ending on something positive. It was clearly a robust Director-style test-out moment, designed to see whether someone who claimed to help others stand up to tough questions could withstand one himself. My reply must have been all right, as this same expert went on to book me to run a session with his group shortly afterwards. He subsequently gave me one of the most glowing testimonials I've ever had and, at his own instigation, sent it around to all his fellow leaders in the organization. He had been satisfied that I could help his organization and its members perform better. As a Director personality, that's what really mattered to him!

So, be ready to have to run an assault course of questions with those in the Director category – especially if there's a watching audience for them to impress. But if you show Directors how you can make them and their organizations perform better, then they can go on to become your new ambassadors – albeit not always particularly diplomatic ones!

2. THE THINKER – who Tony Alessandra labels "The Great Analyser"

These are task-orientated introverts. However be aware that if they do get to or close to the top, like Bill Gates, they can sometimes portray themselves as less introverted because their own analysis suggests they need to appear more outgoing in a leadership role.

Accuracy and detail are important to Thinkers. They are more concerned with getting the job done properly the first time round than with anything else. They tend to focus more on the task itself than the people involved in it. I remember running a series of sessions for some very clever technicians who worked in a kind of high-tech call centre where they had to field client calls when things went wrong with their complex global electronic network. The technicians, mostly in the Thinker category, were clearly good at sorting out the problems – though this often took some time. But they were not so good at keeping the clients reassured while they were waiting for their problem to be sorted. The techies would focus so intently on solving the client's problem that they often didn't concern themselves with keeping the client informed during the process.

I designed a learning-by-doing course to get them to give better responses to the callers, to keep them calm and reassured while the problems were being sorted. I remember one of the participants turning up for the first day of the course, after having clearly had a frustrating time earlier that morning with what he regarded as an impossible client. He stepped into the room and, talking to no one in particular, declared emphatically "I hate people!" So we weren't dealing with Mr Sunshine. However, he and the other Thinker types actually loved the idea of analysing different kinds of people and connecting with them in different ways. The Thinker who supposedly hated people became the prize-winning improver – because he thought deeply about how to get better.

Thinkers don't want to be rushed into making decisions. They like time to reflect while utilizing their analytical skills. They will only feel comfortable making a decision when absolutely satisfied that all their concerns have been covered. Remember this as Bill Gates is carefully quizzing you.

When answering a Thinker's questions, be aware that they want very specific, detailed information and a methodical approach with evidence and proof. Thinkers don't typically exhibit sparkling personalities, but they can be deeply insightful.

The person I've interviewed more times than anyone else on the planet is the one-time solicitor John Howard – who went on to become the second longest-serving Australian Prime Minister. Like many lawyers with a strong grasp of detail, John Howard is a classic Thinker. I clocked up my large interview tally with him during the first of his two stints as Opposition Leader in the Australian Parliament – often recording conversations with him late at night between voting rounds or as I trailed around Australia with him on his campaign travels. He was quietly likeable but often described (rather unfairly) as dour. However, from my perspective and the view of some of my fellow reporters, he made an excellent interviewee. This was because of his impressive grasp of the detail in the law, budgetary figures and impending legislation – not to mention Australian cricketing history. As a result, John Howard was a wizard at coming up with fresh angles on running political stories, which is what political correspondents need. He would regularly provide some useful detail or idea that would help me take a story further – and win an interview slot on the current affairs programmes I was working for. Even though John Howard interviews could be a touch low on emotional content, they often contained elements of great answers as they involved groundbreaking thoughts that took political debates in new directions.

John Howard also threw himself into the challenge of doing devil's advocate interviews, which are a bit like playing a game of chess – where the interviewee has to think ahead in order to avoid saying something that won't stand up to immediate rigorous scrutiny. He tended to be an enthusiastic interviewee, willing to have a shot at challenging subjects. Thinkers don't need to be excessively exciting to be supremely useful! And you can connect with them more easily if you take an interest in the results of their enthusiasm for detail.

3. THE SOCIALIZER – who Tony Alessandra labels "The Great Talker"

These are extroverts with a strong relationship orientation. They are highly expressive. They like people. They enjoy talking about themselves and about you. Socializers tend to be strongly motivated and thrive on achievement gained through people. They enjoy having a sense of influence.

Socializers like to organize teams to accomplish tasks. They can be highly imaginative, energetic and conceptual.

In communication terms, the Socializer can be most influenced by testimonials and stories that show the results of other people's experiences. So, picking the right fascinating examples is especially important when you're answering questions from a Socializer.

Let me tell you about my encounter with the big-personality Socializer, Brian Mulroney, when he was Prime Minister of Canada. It was in Munich in 1992 during the German-hosted summit of the world's richest industrialized economies, known as the Group of Seven nations.

Brian Mulroney held a media conference on the last day of the summit and, with no Australian leader there to interview, I wanted to nab him. But while Mr Mulroney was away from home, a big domestic issue had blown up about separatists in Quebec seeking independence from the rest of Canada, and he spent almost the whole of his media conference fielding questions about this subject, which was of much less interest to the outside world. Because the topic was largely of concern just to the Canadian media, journalists from other countries were physically locked out of the room while it was addressed.

Eventually the doors opened and the Canadian reporters rushed out to file their stories. I strode up to Mr Mulroney and semiseriously complained that Canada had locked Australia – a fellow member of the Commonwealth – out of its press conference.

As a Socializer always up for a chat, he disarmingly asked me if I knew Bob Hawke, the then Australian Prime Minister, who he had met at other international gatherings. His question was right up my street, as I had been covering Mr Hawke's career at close range from Canberra and on his travels around Australia during much of his prime ministership. Bob Hawke is the kind of larger-than-life quintessentially Australian larrikin whose disregard for conventional norms means that everyone who meets him has a story about him. So we exchanged Hawke stories and he then said that on the basis that I knew Mr Hawke he would grant me a one-to-one interview, which he did – giving generously of his time and thoughts about the world summit.

The way to connect with Socializers like Brian Mulroney is to work on the fact that they can't resist telling and listening to stories. So make sure you include engrossing stories and captivating real-life examples as a key part of your great answers to them. Remember this when you answer Bill Clinton's questions.

4. THE RELATER – who Tony Alessandra labels "The Great Helper"

These are people-orientated introverts. They are slow-paced, quiet types who are most concerned about being liked by others and getting along as part of a team.

Relaters do not want to be rushed and will become uneasy if you talk too quickly or insist on rapid decisions. The Relater values the opinions of others and gaining their approval.

In answering their questions Relaters want you to be patient, warm and friendly; to slowly emphasize important points and to highlight any positives for those working with them, as they're sensitive to the needs of others.

Relators don't end up in the limelight as much as other types, so there aren't many of them on the public stage to point to. You might put the former American President, Jimmy Carter, in this category. He came to prominence in unusual circumstances, when the United States wanted to turn to a warmer, more friendly character in the White House – after the traumas associated with the ruthlessly tyrannical Richard Nixon, whose presidency became mired in scandal. Jimmy Carter certainly had the Relater's tendency to be overtly concerned about the well-being of others, which was part of his initial appeal and gave him the patience to become a Middle East peace broker.

I once had a low-key but memorably pleasant encounter with the other relatively well-known Relater mentioned earlier – John Major – after asking him for an interview when he was British Prime Minister. He politely apologized, saying he didn't have time. What was memorable about the moment was that he was so nice about it. It was one of the most warmly and sensitively delivered interview knock-backs I've ever had from a political leader who, as a breed, aren't that fussed about disappointing a reporter from another country.

A key thing to remember with Relaters is that they very much care about the impact they have on others. So when it comes to answering their questions, if you can hit the "What's In It For Those Around Them" factor, you will increase your chances of getting the response you want. Remember that when John Major is asking you questions about the water project.

Giving the right stuff to the right person

Now of course everybody you will ever be answering questions from is a unique individual – so they won't all fit precisely into one of these four categories. Some will contain a mix of characteristics, which will naturally cross the borders of the personality types that Tony Alessandra has defined. For example, having observed Barack Obama closely through the lens of the international media, I find elements of his personality and behaviour range across all the four categories. Perhaps it's this balance that contributes towards making him an impressive communicator.

And when you seek to identify which category suits you most, you may find yourself torn between different ones. To further enhance your question-answering prowess and to better understand yourself and others, it's well worth studying Tony Alessandra's website material.[1]

Whether your questioner fits easily into a single category, or is harder to define, isn't absolutely critical when it comes to your great individualized answers. To maximize your success, what's important is the fundamental underlying point that in one-to-one conversations it is helpful to shape your answers to best appeal to that particular questioner. So, finding out more about your questioners in advance and selecting the most appropriate elements from your material for them is worth factoring into your preparations and performance.

Whether you're dealing with Vladimir Putin, Bill Clinton, Bill Gates, John Major or Fred or Frederika from the accounts department, there's great value in ensuring that your answers are formulated and delivered in the way that will best satisfy and impress them – and help you move towards that win/win outcome you're seeking.

---

[1]   You can find more detail about Tony Alessandra's classification of personality styles at: www.alessandra.com.

PART TWO

USING YOUR NEW TOOLS

By this stage you're hopefully discovering that something amazing takes place when you focus intently on the workplace question and answer process and when you are equipped with the golden formulae among other tools.

You are probably starting to view the answering of questions in a whole new light, and are therefore spotting certain things in verbal encounters that you've never noticed before.

You are also possibly noticing when someone uses one of the golden formulae effectively in their answers.

In Part Two, you can expect to accelerate your move towards mastery of the question and answer. This is where I will help you focus on using your new tools in a variety of specific workplace situations, including:

- giving great answers in sales-oriented conversations with prospects who haven't yet bought from or bought into your organization;

- questions from existing clients who have already bought something from you or your company, where things may not have gone as smoothly as hoped;

- answering those demanding questions from the boss and other workplace colleagues;

- giving answers in a variety of situations such as job interviews, appraisals, price negotiations, meetings, events, media interviews and at those institutions which ask really tough questions if things go wrong – tribunals, inquiries, parliamentary committees and courts.

These upcoming chapters will specifically get you ready for whatever tough conversations your career throws at you from now on.

So far, you have learned how to stop the opponents scoring easily against you – or learned to extinguish the fire.

You are heading towards the point where you can field a tough question as if it were a rugby ball at one end of the field, rapidly carrying it to the other end and scoring – maybe even to massive applause.

Hopefully you have already been playing well with anything you've tried out from the book so far. But however it has been going, as an inspirational sporting coach might tell you: Your best is yet to come!

Chapter 10

GREAT ANSWERS FOR PROSPECTS

There's a thought-provoking sales expert in the professional-speaking world who typically interacts with his audiences like this: "Put your hand in the air if you're in sales!"

As he speaks to business-focused audiences, a number of hands typically go up. But quite a lot of hands remain still.

He then has a provocative message for those who didn't move. He says they were wrong not to have raised their hands. Why? Because he insists that everyone in business is involved in sales in one way or another – or they should be.

The speaker is Steve Clarke.[1] He has a powerful realistic point – relevant to anyone who can get questions about potential future business.

Think about it. If you're running your own company or working in someone else's, there are times when you're going to be in a position to influence sales – whether you're officially on the sales team or not.

---

[1]   There's more on Steve Clarke's approach to sales at: www.eurekasales.co.uk.

You need to be aware that sales success is vital to the ongoing health, and in fact survival, of your organization.

Even if you're a public servant or a charity worker, your organization is probably dependent in some way on people outside it effectively buying in to the value of the services it provides. If no one's prepared to do business with an organization, then you'll end up needing a new job.

So there's every reason to take a healthy interest in the sales side – whatever part of the business you're in. That means being able to deal effectively with sales-related questions.

When you're in professional conversations with prospects – those who might be interested at some stage in buying into what you or your organization have to offer – there are vital questions you should be prepared for.

The toughest of these questions are what people in the world of sales call "objections" – where the prospect asks questions or makes comments suggesting there's an impediment preventing them from agreeing with the proposed solution or product you put forward.

Instead of thinking of these as "objections", it's better to regard them more positively – as "further opportunities" to give additional information, a wider perspective or a refined message. The good news when people are providing you with these "further opportunity" moments is that they're demonstrating how they are engaged with and thinking about the product or service you are suggesting. That's a big plus.

The other question, which arises before you get near any "further opportunity" phase, is the initial "gateway" inquiry when you meet people who may ultimately turn out to be potential customers. It's the "What do you do?" question. We'll deal with this question first, as absolutely everybody gets this one and needs to deal with it supremely well.

Be ready for that "what do you do?" question

The "What do you do?" question is simple, obvious and is asked time and time again. Nonetheless, it's a question many find excruciatingly difficult to answer.

It may not seem like a tough question. And unless you're a secret agent or an undercover secret shopper who can't reveal your true occupation, it shouldn't be that hard. But lots of people do badly on the "What do you do?" test.

For example, I work with a lot of accountants through communications-boosting master classes and the initial answer they often give is: "I'm just another boring accountant." This is not captivating or inspiring. And it's an answer that, while perhaps slightly commendable for its self-deprecation, is hardly going to get people knocking at their door eager to become new clients.

Apart from needing to be more positive, the answer needs to be something that lodges in the memory of the asker. An impressive answer to the "What do you do?" question will stick like chewing gum on a shoe – and be far more welcome!

If you don't answer the question well and it doesn't remain in the asker's brain, the eventual order for the goods or services that your organization offers is likely to go to someone they met in a similar line of work who gave a more enlightening, more exciting and more memorable answer.

When people inquire what you and your organization do, how you portray it will influence the person who posed the question. If it's powerful enough, the essence of your answer will be passed on to others.

At the time of inquiring, the asker may not personally need the particular goods or services you and your organization provide. But at some point that can change. And even more likely, the asker may come across someone else – inside or outside their workplace – who needs exactly what your organization offers. If your answer hasn't enthused and hasn't stuck, then it won't be you or your organization that benefits.

There's a vital underlying principle behind dealing effectively with the "What do you do?" and the "further opportunity" questions from prospects.

The following scenario shows what needs to be at the heart of your approach in responding to these questions in order to succeed…

Selling digital music to cave dwellers

For the next few minutes please – as they say in the world of theatre – suspend disbelief. Put reality checks on hold and let yourself run with this scenario as if it were really happening.

Picture yourself working for a company that manufactures digital music players seeking to compete with the Apple iPod. Your company's research and development team has so many brilliant people in the "Thinker" personality category that apart from designing fantastic music players they have, in their lunch breaks, also invented a time machine. An important aspect of the time machine is that it has an amazing portable translation device that allows the time traveller to communicate with all those they meet on their journeys, whatever period they inhabit.

The inventors of the time machine want someone to take part in its initial trial. Because the machine could put the time traveller in challenging situations with dangerous people, the inventors say the person to test it out should be someone who is really good at connecting with others and answering their potentially tough questions. They know you've read a chunk of this book, so they offer the time machine test-pilot role to you. Before you can stop yourself, you say "Yes".

The research team sets the date selection dial on the time machine to the Stone Age – 10,000 years ago. You get in. The machine works magically.

When you step out, it's early evening and you're in the midst of a tribe of bedraggled, tired-looking cavemen and cavewomen partly covered in grubby skins and furs. They're assembled around a dying campfire and are half-heartedly sharpening their flintstone weapons with other stones outside their cave. They appear tense and grim – as if they've had a really hard day, as part of a really hard life.

The cave folk are naturally a bit shocked by the arrival of you and your time machine, and they don't look happy to see you. You note that some of them are munching aggressively on barbecued meat from the bones of what looks like the carcass of a woolly mammoth in the embers of their fire. Cave children are having a kind of sword fight around the carcass with mammoth tusks. A couple of distraught-looking cave parents are trying unsuccessfully to keep the fracas under control.

Some of the bigger, tougher-looking cavemen then pick up their clubs and come towards you, holding their weapons in the air. As you study them and survey the scene around the mammoth carcass you do what any self-respecting employee in a digital music player company would do in the circumstances: you wonder if you can interest them in owning some digital music players. You are hopeful the little machines would help them relax and enjoy life more.

Obviously the cave people don't have any money or credit cards. But you leap to the idea that their "payment", if you make the "sale", could be through getting their co-operation for the movie rights to a documentary about their progress as they come to grips with playing the most soothing of modern music on the devices. You envisage that such a movie would be a massive hit – and be something that could boost digital music player sales back in your normal time period. And some of the movie highlights could be used in advertisements.

However, you have a problem. You didn't bring any of the digital music players with you to demonstrate. Nonetheless you're confident that – if you can get the cave people interested – the innovative research team would come back in the time machine with a film crew and make the delivery.

Your immediate challenge is to come up with convincing answers to likely cave folk questions, such as: "Why on earth would we want this thing you call a digital music player and put strange things around our ears?" and "What's the point of something like this that won't help us catch more mammoths?"

What do you include in your answers? Do you tell them how the digital technology works? Do you explain that your product involves state-of-the-art science and outline how it follows on from the history of music-playing inventions from the record player to the cassette to the compact disc? Do you tell them how hard the people at the digital music player factory work in order to make such fantastic products?

Here's hoping you don't. Fascinating though all these things may be to some present-day music technology enthusiasts, they won't be of much interest or make much sense to the cave people as they don't have any idea yet what a digital music player – or modern music – is.

If you've got a good sales approach you won't get stuck talking about the processes and effort involved in making your products.

Initially it would be good to ask some questions to increase your understanding of their cave-dwelling lives and build some rapport with them to dissipate their aggression. In particular you should ask some questions about how difficult it is to catch mammoths, how much of a strain it is to bring up well-behaved cave children, and how hard it is to properly relax after a tough day of mammoth hunting.

When you've heard their answers you tell the cave folk how you can provide them with something that's highly relaxing and pleasant to listen to and how it can make them feel ever so calm and relaxed, whatever the pressures around them. And you can tell them that there's evidence – from the time and place where you were sent – that if people are nicely relaxed they're better placed to carry out their tasks and more likely to be successful. So your music could get them in a better state of mind to become better and happier mammoth hunters.

Focus on the benefits

If you took this route you would find yourself doing what great salespeople everywhere do: focusing on the *benefits* that would result from your product rather than its detailed features. In the cave people's case you can't expect them to fully understand the features of your company's product or how it works. But if you paint the right pictures in their minds they'll be able to understand the benefits.

So whether you're selling digital music players to cave dwellers or the latest generation of mobile phones to today's teenagers, you need to focus your sales-oriented answers on what your prospects would gain by having them.

Unsuccessful salespeople lose interest from potential buyers by giving too much detail on the wrong things. Unless there's a particular reason to know, the normal prospect isn't going to be all that fascinated by details of production processes or anything about the workers making the products. They'll be interested in how the product will benefit them or reduce their pain.

So, in line with our imagined experience with the cave people, your answers about your organization's offerings should focus on the *positive effect* they will have on the lives of the would-be buyers.

This applies to both the "further opportunity" questions as well as your answer to the "What do you do?" question.

With pretty much all questions from prospects, "What's In It For Me?" should be at the heart of your message.

Asking great questions paves the way for giving great answers

There is a profoundly true saying in the sales world that people buy from people.

In order for sales to happen smoothly and for the best win/win outcomes, you need to know key things about your prospects and the prospects in turn need to know key things about what you can do for them.

As far as possible, early on focus on what you need to know about them. This is where it's good to remember that you have two ears and one mouth, and that using them in proportion during your conversations is advantageous.

You need to establish what it is out of all your offerings that can potentially be most useful to them. The key to discovering this can be found by asking more about them.

In the scenario with the cave people, you naturally had to know something about their lives before you could realistically convey how your digital music players could positively change things by helping them relax and get in a better state of mind to perform their hunting role.

Make sure you're asking the "What do you do?" question. But you also need to find their pain points. What is it that they have difficulty with – or that could potentially work better?

This is the way you can then determine, out of everything that you could potentially offer, what's going to be the most helpful to the prospect. It's where the potential win/win lies between the two of you.

Your great questions and subsequent great answers can help you and your prospects find out if you can play a part in reducing or eliminating their pain.

Guidance on that "what do you do?" question

Amidst finding out about your prospect, you also must have great ready-made answers for that highly predictable "What do you do?" question. This question presents you with the ultimate marketing opportunity and you need to be ready for it.

Let's go back to those not-so-forthcoming accountants who struggled with the question. One of the things they would say as they explained why they found it difficult was: "There's nothing interesting about me." The trouble with this kind of answer is that some people will actually believe it. Sadly, these particular accountants had begun to believe it themselves. This was despite the fact that they worked for one of the very large accountancy firms involved in all sorts of fascinating projects that hold exciting possibilities and implications for people's lives.

When I pressed the accountants to reveal more about their work, it turned out that they were involved in far more interesting things than they were prepared to initially admit. They didn't tend to do tax returns for the corner shop – not that this couldn't contain something interesting. But the clients they had were frequently involved in seriously big projects involving millions and sometimes billions of pounds. The accountants needed to keep tabs on, and sometimes actually control, the movement of huge amounts of money in the construction of massive transport infrastructure projects and mega shopping centres – the kind of facilities so many people flock to, which must have something inherently interesting about them.

The accountants were also very focused on the latest changes to taxation law. Therefore, they would know how new tax laws or interpretations of existing tax laws would affect people. How much tax is paid is something of interest to people everywhere.

Some of the accountants also had fascinating specialities. One, for example, was an expert in what they called "matrimonial accountancy", which involves who gets what in divorce cases. They actually had far more engrossing issues to talk about than they realized.

So, before answering the question "What do you do?", you need to think about what it is you do that could potentially be of interest to other people to help formulate your best possible answer.

Discover what's fascinating about your field

When planning your introductory talk, put yourself in the minds of others and ask what are the most interesting and useful aspects of what you do? If you're struggling, ask friends or existing clients or colleagues what you offer that others most appreciate. The benefits of what you can bring has to be the central part of what you include in your business introduction. Those benefits are all the more interesting if you and your organization are the only ones to offer them in some particular way.

So if you're an accountant there's much you can say in terms of the benefits you can bring clients. You need to build answers around hitting their "What's In It For Me?" factor.

For example, you could realistically say things like: "I help businesses manage their affairs more effectively so they can make more profit"; "I help people make sure they're paying the right amount of tax and no more"; or "I assist people going through divorce to come out with the best possible financial arrangements".

Telling people how you can benefit them is a key part of giving great answers to questions from prospects. If ancient cave dwellers could conceivably understand the benefits of a modern-day product without needing to know about the technology or history or hard work that made it possible, then you can do it with present-day people. Just focus on how you and/or your organization can potentially make their lives and/or businesses better.

Answering the elevator question

When people ask what you do, they're effectively seeking what's known as your "elevator pitch". This is what you would tell someone you met on a short journey in an elevator or lift as you travelled between floors. It can have equal applicability to someone you meet at a conference, in a bar or walking along a beach.

If you get it right, it doesn't come over as anything like a "pitch" as such. People don't like being "pitched at" if they're not in a formal pitch process. So I prefer to regard it as an "elevator introduction" or your "verbal business card". It's more a matter of revealing how you make an impact. This gets things heading in a potentially fruitful direction for both of you – either immediately or in a future conversation.

Because time is limited, you need to have a straight-to-the-point elevator introduction ready for the occasion.

You ideally need a short, medium and longer version. That's something like a ten-second version, a thirty-second version and a sixty-second version.

The ten-second version is a headliner when you are on a one-floor elevator ride or in a networking conversation, which requires a succinct introduction. But even in ten seconds you still have the opportunity to say what you can do for others. If they ask for your business card before they get out of the elevator or go to meet the next person, then you've done well! If they call you later, you've done even better!

The thirty-second version is ideal for those informal networking gatherings where it's helpful to give a bit more information to arouse interest and provide a potential hook – by saying something intriguing – to encourage them to ask more. This version is also useful if you have to introduce yourself at the start of one of those exploratory business meetings between two or more firms, where you're getting to know others around the table to see what business or collaboration might be possible.

The sixty-second version is typically for more formal situations. It's like a mini-presentation. It can be used in the official opening part of some networking events, where they allocate a minute for you to stand up and answer the "What do you do?" question. In some places – such as at Business Network International breakfast meetings – they actually time you and a bell or buzzer sounds at the sixty-second mark. It's amazing how much you can pack into a minute – typically more than you originally think – if it's well planned. The aim is to say just enough so that the right people will come up to ask more later.

Never speed through your sixty-second talk. If you have too much packed in, you and your audience are much better served if you take a bit out rather than race through it, which can undermine your authority.

Structuring your self-introduction

Whatever the occasion, you can structure your self-introduction around The First Golden Formula, but you don't need the bridge element.

So think ACDE – answer flowing on to the content of your key message and then the dangle of an example.

Let's try it with our accountants in mind. Here's a draft response to that "What do you do?" question.

Answer/Content of key message: "I'm an accountant specializing in helping clients make more profit, working with manufacturing companies."

Dangle: "For instance…"

Example: "…my team looks over all aspects of their operations from their factories to their head office to see where they can either cut costs or increase their margins. With a typical client we can boost their profits by 7% in the first year. With one clothing manufacturer we took on a couple of years ago we recommended a lot of changes and their first year profit went up by 28.5%."

You can vary the amount of detail you include in the example depending on whether you have time for a shorter or a longer version.

You can hopefully see how, if you were a manufacturer listening to this business introduction, you might be tempted to ask more about the higher profits that were achieved. You may want to find out more detail about how costs are cut and how increased margins are achieved. You may even want to ask if the accountant could visit your office and explore whether it's worth hiring his services.

The introduction, by its nature, doesn't have time to reveal everything. But if you do it well there is enough for the right target to be motivated to want to ask you more.

When it comes to the examples, you can see how it would be helpful to get clearance from some delighted clients to allow you to talk about certain non-sensitive aspects of their situation. If you can get this approval then your example becomes all the more credible when you give the actual name of the company to benefit, with their blessing.

It's great if you can have the shorter and longer versions of your self-introduction at least semi-planned. And it's helpful to have a variety of examples, so that you can choose the right one depending on who you're talking to.

You don't want your introduction to look excessively planned – or overly cheesy. I remember a dentist who introduced himself as working at the place where "the science of dentistry meets the magic of your smile". It was memorable but too obviously planned – and kind of sickening at the same time.

The ideal is to deliver your introduction with "planned spontaneity", so that it's practiced enough to be smooth and flowing but not so much so that it sounds over-planned or over-rehearsed. Ideally it should come across in a way that sounds almost as though it just popped into your head.

When you've worked out what you want to say it is well worth doing some practice. Try outs in front of a mirror – or if possible on video with playbacks – are a worthwhile investment of your time. Practice and polish your introduction, ending on different examples for different occasions.

Dealing with those tough sales questions

At some stage after you've met a new prospect and things have progressed well, you may end up in a more focused sales-oriented discussion. This is when the prospect has shown the right "buying signals" to indicate they want to discuss the possibility of purchasing what you have on offer.

If you're not on the official sales team, this may be the time to hand the prospect over to one of the designated sales representatives. But whether this is the right thing to do – or whether you are authorized to carry on more specific business discussions – there are important things to consider about how to frame sales-oriented conversations and how to move things forward.

As a general principle, when you're in the role of a potential seller, what you need to be doing is making it as easy as possible for potential buyers to buy. So instead of "hard-sell" answers, which frequently put buyers off, the seller should be aiming to assist buyers. This is achieved by working in partnership with them – to help them make the right decision for them and their organization. So when it comes to those "objection/further opportunity" questions, it's the seller's role to be as helpful as possible. This can involve providing additional information, suggesting that tentative conclusions need to be rethought, or inviting potential buyers to view a situation from a different or wider perspective.

A productive sales discussion does not come down to an argument. At its best, the seller is guiding the potential buyer towards achieving the aims established in the early part of the conversation – where the seller asked the buyer about their challenge and their requirements.

The ABCDE formula is profoundly useful in sales conversations – but it typically needs to be applied in a gentle way, rather than in a confrontational manner. It's a matter of using the formula to guide the potential buyer in the direction that is in his/her interests rather than to aggressively challenge any reluctance – however irrational you may think it is.

Here's how ABCDE can be deployed in a very simple way.

Prospect: "I don't like the shades of red or green or blue that the product comes in. Why does it come in such a limited range of standard colours?"

The gentle draft answer can be something like this.

Answer: "We have to keep the range of standard colours to a minimum in order to keep the costs down. These three colours proved the most popular in surveys with potential customers."

Bridge: "But what you might be interested to know is…"

Content of key message: "…our company prides itself on seeking to provide exactly what our customers want when it comes to colour schemes. We provide a bespoke service where, for a relatively small amount – less than 5% above the normal cost – the company will do a version in a shade that's as close as we can get to what you require."

Dangle: "A really good example of how that works is…"

Example: "…with a customer we had last month who was redecorating her home. She had already ordered the wallpaper, and wanted the product from us to be exactly the same colour as that wallpaper. We gave a sample of the wallpaper to the production team and they managed to match it exactly. The customer and her family were ecstatic with the result."

So you can imagine that the next question from the prospect after hearing this could be something like:

"How much exactly would it be if I ordered the product in the honeydew green shade that I really want?"

In a low-key way, this kind of use of the ABCDE formula can put the conversation on a highly constructive path.

Answers that bridge in the right direction for your prospects allow you to guide them to the right place to make the best decisions for them – and put you in a position to get the right order with a happy long-term outcome for your prospect and for you.

The same low-key, helpful approach in your answers can also be applied to really tough questions about price. This is where discussions with prospects can either come unstuck or lead the way to great win/win agreements. This is such an important topic that it's considered in a separate chapter – the next one.

Chapter 11

GREAT ANSWERS DURING PRICE NEGOTIATIONS

There's one situation where you should always consider compromise.

It's where you can't get everything exactly your own way.

Alas, as a seller, when you're seeking to reach an agreement on price, getting completely your own way isn't always possible.

It would be a wonderful world for sellers if, every time they sent off their priced proposal, the prospect simply said "Yes".

Of course this can and does happen sometimes. If you've listened carefully to what your prospect requires and have positioned your proposal carefully, so they immediately recognize its value and relevance to them, then a straight "Yes" can be the response.

But often it's rather different. In these cases, if the prospect doesn't just say "No" they typically ask tough questions – questions that usually involve downward pressure on your price.

Be ready for questions like these...

You need to be ready for questions such as:

- "How can you possibly justify that price?"
- "I can get the same thing for two-thirds of that amount elsewhere. Can you match that?"
- "We can only sign the contract if you give us a 10% discount?"
- "Why are you so expensive?"

These are questions which, as discussed in the last chapter, amount to what hardened salespeople call "objections". We now know these are really "further opportunities" for you to deliver great answers in order to point you and your negotiating partner towards a win/win outcome.

Negotiation in itself can be a welcome and necessary thing. If you've ever had to get a reluctant toddler to go to bed – or get a reluctant teenager out of bed – you may know that getting an agreement involving rewards can help make things happen more smoothly and avoid tantrums (on a good day).

To bring about this happy situation you normally need to enter into some form of negotiation. And as a seller, negotiations are more likely to lead you towards a much better outcome if you give great answers to tough price-challenging questions.

There is a stereotyped view of negotiation that it must involve a ruthless, cold-blooded, aggressive approach in order to get the right outcome. This view is misguided in a lot of cases – especially as far as price negotiations are concerned. The approach recommended here is much more positive and much more pleasant, with the aim being a win/win satisfying both parties.

Negotiations over price are far more likely to get the right outcome if conducted like a gentle, sensitive ballroom dance with two partners seeking to find an effective way to become entwined for mutual benefit. This needs a positive approach on behalf of the seller – aimed at solving any joint problems you have to overcome to get an agreement that works for both of you. This positive approach needs to be reflected in great answers for your prospects, however negative their questions may be.

In the conversations along the way, you can judge if the approach of your negotiation partners is so negative that you wouldn't want to do business with them under any circumstances. But if you give a positive lead it can set the right constructive tone and make success a more likely outcome.

Plan your approach for great outcomes

It's much easier to take a positive approach as the seller if you plan your initial proposal, your negotiation position and your potential great answers to their likely questions in advance.

This chapter is naturally focused largely on the great *answers* you need to be giving during price negotiations, but these are of course intertwined with your negotiation strategy and tactics themselves.

Here we will touch on the key principles involved in planning and carrying out effective negotiation – principles which should underpin the great answers that you need to give to make things move in the right direction.

There are some insightful books that are purely on negotiation and if this is a skill you need to concentrate on, then it's well worth reading one of them as well as what's here.[1]

Of course you can't normally get a great win/win outcome if you don't invest time and thought into some careful planning. Negotiation itself has a lot in common with giving great answers. The right preparation is vital in getting the outcome you want. The position you adopt for a negotiation needs to be well thought through – as does the way you communicate it. So, your negotiation plan and your great answers plan should sit together ever so comfortably.

This really is a case like house building, where you have to get the foundations laid properly on solid ground in order to create a structure that stands up and lasts. What follows are some important principles which, if put into practice, will make producing those great answers during the negotiation all the easier.

Key negotiation principles to underpin your great answers

A key part of getting the price negotiation process right is to understand what your potential buyer needs and wants. You can establish that by asking the right questions and listening ever so carefully to the replies. There's a danger of giving a price too soon, before you've established every requirement. The more you know before you come out with your initial offer, the better you can craft it, position it and effectively highlight its merits with your answers to their challenging questions.

---

1   One of the books I recommend on negotiation in business is the exquisitely named *Why Do Smart People Make Such Stupid Mistakes?* by Chris Merrington.

You may have a set list of well-worked-out standard prices, but often the prospect in a negotiation wants something different from the standard or something that involves a combination of the things that you can provide. In these cases it's often a matter of coming up with a package of elements.

One of the important things I've learned is that giving just a single straight take-it-or-leave-it price proposal can be all too easy for the prospect to leave. What's generally better is to offer a range of options with different prices. This aids the process of negotiation and more easily heads you both towards a win/win outcome.

Making gold, silver and bronze offerings

One enlightened approach is to come up with a "gold, silver and bronze" set of options, with different prices for different levels. This gives you flexibility during your negotiation and allows you to consider a lower price without actually backing down. Having a graded set of options means that you have a pre-set structure. So if the price has to be lower, then you can instantly make it clear in your answer what would be taken out of the package as a result.

An essential element of effective negotiation is to make sure that when you're asked for a concession, you only give in a way that ties it to an appropriate concession in return. It's a "something for something" approach. Presenting a series of differently priced options enables you, in the face of downward pressure on price, to move position easily without surrender.

Surrender constitutes just agreeing to a price reduction without any balancing concession. This is dangerous. It can be perceived as indicating that the original price you quoted was unrealistically high and that you were merely seeking to "see what you could get away with".

Shifting price with a corresponding concession underlines the impression that the original prices were properly thought out and that your initial costings deserve to be respected.

The other reason to avoid a concession with nothing in return is that it invites another request for another price drop. If you're asked for a 10% discount and you give it with no corresponding concession in return, there is nothing to stop your negotiation partner from then seeking a further 10% discount – and then another!

Having a well-worked-out set of graded starting options makes it a lot easier to give great answers, because the substance of what you can put forward has already been established. It helps prevent you from giving badly-thought-out answers on the run, which you may live to regret.

What to prepare in advance

Here's what you typically want to have ready in advance of a price discussion:

- A way of setting out your offer/s that makes the value clear – showing the benefits to the prospect.

- A target price.

- A walkaway price below which you won't go – without receiving some offsetting concession. This walkaway price does not have to be overtly disclosed at the outset. But it guides you during your negotiation conversation, so you know what's acceptable to you and what you'll stop yourself settling for.

- A gold, silver and bronze set of options – which can involve additional levels such as gold-plus and silver-minus when dealing with a complicated situation. These options are built around your target price and your walkaway price.

- A way of discounting a package offer in return for a larger bulk deal – if that's of benefit to you.

- A plan for discounting in return for more favourable payment terms, such as a shorter amount of time to pay after the invoice is sent – say 14 days instead of 28 days. Or you could be prepared to discount in return for receiving a chunk of the payment in advance – possibly even all of it.

- A list of potential tough questions and key messages, examples and answers prepared, which draws on all your above preparation.

Having all this in place before any negotiations begin will make it so much easier for you to remain focused on a positive outcome and avoid rash answers.

Putting it into action

Let's see what preparing gold, silver and bronze options in advance can look like in a specific situation. Then we can see how you can use this preparation to give instant, easy-to-formulate answers in your price discussions because you already have your positions worked out in advance.

Imagine you're a chef with a rising profile, a big personality and high aspirations. You've worked in some prominent restaurants and are building a reputation as someone with insightful views about the way food should be prepared. You've been developing your own ways of doing things in the kitchen. You have concocted your own signature dishes, involving ingredients from your own area and your own favourite suppliers. You're establishing an attractive, enticing personal brand around your name, personality and style.

At the moment you're enhancing your celebrity status by working in various places as a so-called guest chef. This is where you temporarily take charge of a kitchen team, for a day or a series of days, and produce your menu and dishes for special events at a restaurant. This enables you to further build your profile and your fan base in the area where you're working. This modern pattern of work allows you time to blog on food issues and build your social media following. You've written a cookbook that's about to come out. This is expected to enhance your reputation as something of a celebrity in the food world.

Things are generally going well for your potentially prosperous future. However, since giving up a regular job with regular hours you have been painfully short of cash as you build your brand.

One day you receive an email from a tough, innovative entrepreneur in the food industry who you've met a couple of times and who purports to be an admirer.

> *Dear X,*
>
> *I'm writing to sound you out about getting involved as a guest chef in my new chain of restaurants (based on my existing restaurant in your city) that I'm setting up with my financial partners.*
>
> *We're keen to bring in carefully selected guest chefs to tour our restaurants, produce menus for special nights and interact with our guests to add to the excitement of the experience. We know this role suits your personality and culinary skills.*

I'm keen to see if you might do this for us on at least one occasion next year and to explore whether it's affordable for us.

I know you have your cookbook coming out soon and if you were to become a roving guest chef for our chain we could use our prestigious dining events to help promote it as part of our arrangement.

If you're interested, it would be good to meet with you over lunch to explore how we could potentially make it work.

Best regards,
Mr Restaurant Entrepreneur

This opportunity is of great interest. It will lead to a lot of questions, which you need to be ready for over that proposed lunch. Given that the entrepreneur has made a reference to "whether it's affordable", you can expect questions that involve downward price pressure. You don't want to be making up figures on the run. So you need to have positions and draft answers ready for that lunchtime discussion.

Let's go through some preparations so your great answers are oven-ready during that lunch.

To keep the arithmetic simple, we will keep expenses like travel and accommodation out of the equation and work on the basis that they would all be covered by the contract covering whatever agreement is reached.

From a negotiation point of view, working on the basis of a day rate may not be your best approach in this kind of situation. It may well be better to make a broader packaged proposal, which avoids day rates and focuses on the outcomes you will achieve for your client. However, for the purposes of having an easy-to-follow

scenario, working with day rates here helps illustrate the importance of the negotiation principles involved.

So let's assume you need to get at least £300 for each working day
and preparation day to make an agreement worthwhile. But you
are aspiring to get £500 a day given your growing profile. This is
what you like to charge for events where you step out of the
kitchen and interact with the diners as part of the deal. You have
a talent for this and know that a lot of chefs are nervous and not
so impressive at conversing entertainingly with restaurant patrons.
So this is somewhere you can add value – as well as promote your
own personal brand and, as the entrepreneur encouragingly suggests, sell your cookbooks as well.

So £500 a day is your target price where you're happy to interact
with diners as part of the deal.

And £330 a day is your bottom-line price where you restrict yourself to just running the kitchen. You decide any offer below this
would be the walk-away point.

But you have some variables to explore. Getting a string of days
working in a restaurant makes it more worthwhile for you than just
doing a one-off single day.

You also note the entrepreneur's reference to being able to
promote your book as part of the exercise. To keep it simple, let's
assume you can make a reasonable profit on your cookbooks if you
sell them for £20 each. You can add to the books' perceived value
by signing them for designated individuals at the events. This
would presumably appeal to the entrepreneur as well. You can
suggest to the entrepreneur that he could have a premium offer,
where the diners who pay extra for their ticket get one of your
cookbooks included. Alternatively, some of your books could be

given to diners whose names are pulled from a hat. You could do the draw yourself, to help build the buzz around your cookbook.

So the cookbooks and your meet-the-diners chats are your variables as you work out a simple gold, silver and bronze package:

- Gold package of £700 per day for running the kitchen, mixing with the diners, giving away ten books and signing them in front of the guests. (This gets you your target of £500 a day for your work and allows you to sell ten books at £20 each.)

- Silver package of £600 per day for running the kitchen, mixing with the diners, giving away five books and signing them in front of the guests. (This gets you your target of £500 a day and allows you to sell five books at £20 each.)

- Bronze package of £350 per day for running the kitchen but not interacting with diners and giving away just one book, which is pre-signed. (This gets you your bottom-line £330 a day and allows you to sell one book at £20.)

With these levels worked out in advance, if you start by putting forward the gold option you can see that you are in a much stronger position to stand up to any pressures for discounts.

You need to avoid accepting any discount on your price unless you get something in return.

The gold package is what you would most want to do. So you need to have good answers ready to show its value.

You can introduce the gold option early in the conversation – and indicate that there are other options available.

Having these other options will help you stick to a position of strength at those moments when the prospect shakes his head from side to side and loudly sucks air into his mouth while indicating that it's all too expensive. Having the silver and bronze options means you have alternatives to simply caving in and accepting a lower price.

You work out that it's worth your while to discount the rates you give by 10% if you get three or more days' work in a row in the same restaurant.

You also give yourself the option to shift the payment terms. You are normally paid within 28 days, but given your pressing cash flow problems it would be well worth your while to bolster your bank account immediately by giving a 5% discount in return for being paid 50% in advance for every day you're booked. And you could accept a 10% discount in return for being paid 100% in advance for every day you're booked.

So if the pressure comes to reduce your prices, you now have somewhere to take the conversation that's in your interest, and you have the base for some great potential answers at the ready.

Putting your preparation into action

You meet Mr Entrepreneur in a private dining room in his restaurant. Naturally the staff have been instructed to make a special effort and you're impressed with the rock star treatment you get and the high standard of food you're offered. Of course you demonstrate your mastery of your subject by making some diplomatic but illuminating comments about the food along the way. You also take the opportunity to discuss how your social media following is accelerating and how your cookbook is expected to take your profile to new heights.

As the chit-chat continues, Mr Entrepreneur tells you more about his expansion plans for his chain and he paints a glowing picture of future success and prosperity. You're thinking to yourself that being a roving guest chef for this operation could be just the thing for you. But for tactical reasons you stop yourself from looking excessively enthusiastic early in the conversation.

Halfway through the meal it's crunch time. You're asked about how much you would need to be rewarded for each day as a guest chef in the chain. You set out your gold option and Mr Entrepreneur listens carefully. He does indeed look incredulous when you mention the daily rate of £500, which he knows is above the general market rate.

And sure enough he asks you, as you anticipated that he might: "How on earth could you possibly justify that price to my financiers?"

You naturally have your answer prepared with the help of the ABCDE formula.

Answer: "That's easy, as I'm offering high value that will increase the traffic at your restaurants."

Bridge: "What your financiers need to take into account is…"

Content of your key message: "…that when my cookbook comes out shortly, my profile will become way higher than it is now. So without being too immodest or optimistic, I expect that publicizing the special evenings when I'm the guest chef will make a significant increase to the number of patrons you will draw in."

Dangle: "Bear in mind that…"

Example: "…my publisher is expecting that the cookbook will be reviewed in all the major papers and leading gourmet magazines. So we can be confident as a result of these reviews that on nights when we have special events it will draw in readers who want to try some of the dishes for themselves."

Mr Entrepreneur appears impressed but is trying not to look too carried away. He follows up with: "I can get some good chefs for half the price you're asking. Can you compete with that?"

Again you have an ABCDE response planned.

Answer: "Well, I could only do a rate like that on a very restricted basis."

Bridge: "What you and your financiers would need to factor in is that…"

Content of key message: "…on the basis you suggest I would only be able to do my part on less attractive terms."

Dangle: "For example…"

Example: "…my financial advisor says I should only do a guest chef slot on that kind of rate if it means dealing with just the cooking side, without any other responsibilities. So it couldn't involve any table tours and instead of offering twenty cookbooks on each night I could only afford to give one cookbook."

This produces exactly the effect you wanted. Mr Entrepreneur looks as if he's just sucked a particularly sour lemon. He can see that his plans to capitalize on the pulling power of your personality wouldn't work so well under that arrangement.

Later in the conversation Mr Entrepreneur excuses himself for a short while, saying that he needs to have a telephone conversation with the biggest of his financiers. After returning and doing some tapping on his calculator, he goes back to the topic of your gold offer.

"What if we went with your original proposal of doing the walk-abouts and providing the ten books with the book signings, but we took 10% off your £700 a day figure to make it more acceptable to my financiers?"

This is your turn to look unimpressed. But you can still keep the negotiation on track by shifting to your prepared position about doing a bulk deal.

Answer: "There's one way I can see that this could possibly be made to work."

Bridge: "What you would need to do would be…"

Content: "…to give me three or more days in a row at the venue instead of a single night at that rate."

Dangle: "So that would mean…"

Example: "…you would get your 10% discount in return for putting on our special menu three days in a row at the same restaurant. Obviously when we are doing three days in a row you will have more tickets to sell, but I could help with that."

At this point you dangle an additional example: "For instance, ahead of the occasions when we have three successive days in the one restaurant I could help your ticket sales if you could offer a discount code to my Twitter followers who wanted to come. I would help publicize the event through social media and be able to promote it as a special offer for my followers, which would be good for you, me and your financiers."

Let's assume this goes down well with Mr Entrepreneur, who expresses enthusiasm for the idea of collaboration whereby you, he and his financiers are seeking to promote his restaurant events for mutual benefit.

But tough negotiators often insist that they have to report back to other parties to get approval, a tactic known as "absent authority". So Mr Entrepreneur insists at the end of the meal that he will need to outline what you discussed with his financiers and then get back to you with an answer.

The next day the phone rings. Mr Entrepreneur says he has good and bad news. The good news is that his colleagues are keen on the idea of accepting what is effectively your gold offer with that 10% discount for doing it three days in a row – and they would be delighted to give you a special discount code for your Twitter followers.

However, Mr Entrepreneur adds that there is just one thing to consider. He said he was keen to support your amended proposal and to offer you three specific days near the start of next year with a view to offering more, providing the evenings worked out as successfully as they expected. But, he adds ominously, the total figure is still higher than his financiers had in mind and in order to proceed they would need an additional 10% off the total price to make it happen.

Of course your pre-thought-out strategy allows a mechanism for this!

You say: "I can discuss that offer with my financial advisor provided that the contract stipulates you pay 100% in advance to secure each set of three days, instead of the normal payment 28 days after the event."

You can hear Mr Entrepreneur sucking in air through his teeth. But then he says: "If you put that in your draft contract, I will get back to you with an answer within 24 hours."

Your financial advisor endorses the plan to send the proposed contract later in the day. It comes back on your computer screen, signed, the next morning. The following day you have the amount you discussed sitting in your bank account earning interest immediately, and three great days of profile-enhancing work in your diary for next year to look forward to. You're confident that some of your Twitter followers will be ecstatic to use that special discount code to come and see you and savour your signature dishes. And you're delighted that some of them will walk away with a signed copy of your cookbook to show their friends, who might buy it too.

You can hopefully see how much easier the advance preparation including gold, silver and bronze tiers can make your price negotiation conversations, helping you to construct pre-thought-out answers to predictable questions.

Conversations about price can become heated, tense and nasty. But when you have positive answers worked out in advance – based on a well-crafted foundation – it makes it so much easier to counter the negative questions aimed at pushing down your prices.

Planned positive answers can help move all negotiating partners towards a win/win outcome. They also keep things more civilized than they might otherwise be – which bodes well for renewing contracts and expanding future arrangements.

Chapter 12

GREAT ANSWERS FOR CLIENTS

When things are going well, answering tough questions from existing clients can be a lot easier than answering tough questions from new prospects who are yet to buy anything from you. But when things are going badly, answering tough questions from existing clients can be a lot harder.

This chapter will look at responding to tough questions from clients both when things are going relatively well and badly.

It will deal with answers in good moments, when you need to design responses to enhance your business relationships with existing clients. And it will deal with answers in challenging moments, when you need to design responses aimed at protecting – or possibly even saving – those business relationships. This includes those hopefully rare occasions when you get questions from clients who rightly or wrongly think that whatever has gone wrong is entirely your fault.

Ideally, most conversations you have with clients will be after you have already impressed, wowed and delighted them with what you and/or your company has done or started doing for them. This can put you in a strong position, in contrast to conversations you have with them while they are a prospect – when you can rightly be perceived as merely an untested potential supplier, with no track record upon which to demonstrate your ability to help them.

Great answers that help build high-level client partnerships

The difference between being questioned by a prospect and a client can be a bit like the difference between answering questions at a job interview and answering questions when you've already secured the post and are performing in the workplace, hopefully doing great things. I say "a bit like" advisedly, because if you play your cards right in your professional conversations, the relationship with a client can actually get to a stage where it's far superior to any relationship with an employer. Ideally, with some clients you end up going way beyond a de facto employee–employer relationship and into the high-level partnership zone. This is then reflected in the way you answer questions, as well as in the rewards that can flow to you and your client.

When things go swimmingly with a client you can get to the point where you are more like a star consultant than a supplier. In such cases, you can be called upon to help the client deal with particular problems or take charge of specific projects where they perceive that you are more capable than they are of tackling their challenge or at least shining light on it.

In some ideal cases you can go a big step beyond acting in the capacity of a consultant and become a trusted advisor. In such situations you are there to help your client in a special way, where you are positioned more as a cherished partner than a mere supplier. Even if you're selling them goods rather than services, your advice on what they need and how to utilize it can put you in a position where you're their highly esteemed "go to" person in your area because of your expertise, and because they want that expertise on tap.

At such times you may find yourself effectively taking part in an unusual kind of ballroom dance, where you as a supplier are actually leading the client. To get to this position you need to be very much inside the client's mind and be aware of their challenges. This can involve asking a lot of questions along the way. This enables you to include in your answers recommendations that are tailored to meet the client's requirements and best serve their interests.

Answering questions in the best possible way as your business relationships develop can help elevate you to that trusted advisor position, which can be highly beneficial for both you and your clients.

Initially in this chapter we will look at questions in marketing-orientated situations, where you can build on the work you've already done with the client by pro-actively focusing some conversations on what you can do for your client in the future.

These can involve questions about problems the client has – which, if you give the right answers, can lead to future programmes of work or product sales the client may be interested in and benefit from. In these cases there are similarities between your answers to these questions and those that we considered in the last two chapters concerning questions from prospects and in price negotiations. However, once you have established a client relationship – and are being paid for your efforts or your products – you are in a potentially stronger situation from the one you are in with prospects. In client relationships you are demonstrating what you can do, not just promising what you hope to do in the future. In these cases you can effectively be on your client's team – and this can be reflected in the way you give your answers.

Positive responses to client worries

Even when you get challenging questions about something that has disappointed your client, you can potentially turn an apparently negative situation into the win/win of a solution for your client and a positive business opportunity for your company.

Here you can draw on the inspiring optimism underlying that proverb: "What you do when life hands you lemons? – Make lemonade!"

First we will look at what might be classed as relatively small client challenges, which don't involve major problems or strong negative emotions. We're looking here at what amount to annoyances and worries for the client, rather than catastrophes. If you put forward the right solutions, these annoyances and worries can be like that grit in the oyster which helps produce the pearl.

In these cases you can apply the ABCDE formula to shift the conversation in a more positive and productive direction, off the back of a question about a negative situation.

Let's take a look at how this can work.

Suppose you're working in a training firm that has just been running a hands-on safety course for a chemical company. The course has concentrated on preventing low-scale accidents on the factory floor – and dealing with relatively small injuries like minor cuts, bruises and burns if they happen. From your perspective, the course has gone really well. The participants have learned useful techniques and said positive things about how valuable the day has been for them. These are broadly reflected in the responses on the feedback forms that you've just glanced at before sitting down for a post-session chat with your client over a glass of something. The two of you start sifting through the forms in more detail and they're generally glowing.

However, there is one feedback form question where the answers make unsettling reading for your client. The responses indicate that a significant number of the participants, having been focused all day on minor accidents and injuries, have actually now become more worried that they are not adequately prepared for the nightmare of a major chemical explosion. The client says that this is something that keeps her awake at night as well, before asking you if you are disappointed with the results on this question.

Great answers to prompt positive client action

You can choose to view this question – uncomfortable though it is – as an opportunity to interest the client in one of your training firm's much larger and more ambitious offerings. This offering is a major experiential session that involves simulating a chemical explosion and deploying role-play actors to portray seriously injured victims in the chaos that follows. It provides a learning-by-doing experience that helps companies in the management and practicalities of coping with a major disaster.

Here's how you can put together an ABCDE response to that question about whether you're disappointed by the concerns of participants regarding their perceived readiness to cope with a large-scale chemical explosion.

Answer: "Not really. We've understandably had this kind of response before from participants when their team has been focusing all day on minor safety matters to the extent that they end up with a heightened state of awareness about what can go wrong. As a result, they often end up with a higher level of anxiety about how they would cope – or not cope – with a large-scale explosion."

Bridge: "What we can do is run a programme that addresses the team members' concerns and inspires them to increase their preparedness to deal effectively with a major disaster."

Content of key message: "We have a sophisticated training session involving role-play actors, where we simulate a major disaster and test out the company's response plans for dealing with it. There are two major benefits of an exercise like this. The first one is obvious – the team ends up being better equipped and practiced to manage in the event of a catastrophe, minimize suffering and deal with large-scale injuries if the worst happens. The second important, but less obvious, benefit is that by channelling everyone's attention on just how horrendous the situation would be for real in a major chemical explosion, it focuses your team's energies on doing all the things you need to do to ensure that, as far as humanly possible, the worst never happens. Once a team has been through the exercise they are more highly motivated than ever to ensure they have – and maintain – the best possible prevention measures."

Dangle: "A really good example of this kind of exercise is one we have just run…"

Example: "…with another major chemical company that was worried that the kind of massive explosion which took place in Bhopal in India in 1984 could happen to them. You may recall that in the Bhopal tragedy over half a million people were exposed to poisonous gas and other dangerous chemicals, with thousands dying and ongoing suffering for thousands more, along with serious birth defects in future generations. The Bhopal situation is about as horrendous as things can get in the chemical industry, and the obvious benefit of our simulated exercise was that the team members who took part all felt much better able to cope in future because everyone got to practice their own individual roles in the plan for coping with a big emergency.

One of the most interesting and useful factors was that even though it was a simulated exercise, people taking part still felt very emotional about the feigned deaths and injuries to their colleagues and to passers-by outside the factory. So afterwards they felt that the exercise had effectively prepared them for the challenge of having to cope with their own personal emotional responses, while at the same time taking practical measures to help the injured and deal with the explosion. The other thing was that by getting practice in dealing with this horrendous worst-case scenario, they all found themselves being far more focused on prevention measures. Dealing with the actors who appeared to be suffering serious injuries, with the help of good movie-style make-up, concentrated the team's mind on enhancing the safety culture of the company. So they all agreed that, as a result of preparing for the worst, they had actually made it less likely to happen. This made everyone involved in the exercise feel justifiably better equipped and safer."

You can imagine that this kind of detailed, colourful and comprehensive answer could then invite all sorts of questions from the client about how such an emergency planning exercise could be run at their factory. So, drawing on the ABCDE formula can shift the client conversation in a much more positive pro-active direction for both questioner and answerer. It can help put you in the trusted advisor zone and enable you and your client to go beyond focusing on the problem to discussing a solution which is mutually beneficial.

Dealing with tough client questions when something's gone badly wrong

Now let's look at tough questions surrounding a situation where something serious has gone wrong with what you have provided for your client – and you're getting tough questions as a result. These questions are based on the premise that it's your fault and involve asking what you're going to do about it.

Let's suppose that the chemical company went ahead and booked a series of three simulated emergency training days with you in order to improve their preparedness for coping with a disaster. You've been in charge of setting up the contract to run the exercises, although you have delegated to a colleague, David, the responsibility of managing the programme on the client's premises on the three big days. A key part of the simulated explosion programme involves role-play actors from your company who pretend to be injured – screaming in agony at times where appropriate to conjure up the right terrifying atmosphere – as part of the exercise.

Unfortunately, a real injury occurs during the first training exercise. While fleeing the factory after the simulated explosion one of the participants from the chemical company, George, tripped over one of your role-play actors, Cyril, while he was lying on the floor near an exit feigning injury. Both George and Cyril were, quite properly, immediately sidelined from the exercise by David. Cyril, who has first aid qualifications, treated George's cuts. David wrote up a report on the accident, got statements from the participants who witnessed the fall, and recorded the details in an accident log. As a precautionary measure George is taken for a medical check-up. Cyril and David later tell you what has happened and say you can expect a phone call from the client, Petra. They predict that she will have some tough questions to ask, even though you all agree that the right steps were taken immediately after the accident.

You do indeed get the predicted call from Petra. She tells you that, contrary to first appearances, George was more seriously injured than had originally been thought. She says the doctor diagnosed that in addition to the cuts, George had concussion and would need to be off work for at least two weeks. This was a problem, because George plays a key role in managing the chemical production process. Petra then asks if your training firm will take full responsibility for the accident and pay compensation to the injured George and to her company.

1. Establish the facts

This is a difficult question. You are not a lawyer, you are not absolutely certain of all the surrounding facts yet, and your company hasn't had the benefit of any legal advice at the time you take Petra's call. You are aware that companies can look bad in the eyes of their clients and the public if they are slow and grudging to admit responsibility and make amends. You know that your company has a legal duty of care to those taking part in your training exercises on their premises. So you have a fine line to tread between showing sympathy for the injured George and to your client while simultaneously not admitting any unnecessary liability without legal advice.

When something bad has happened to your client, it's important to establish the facts so you, with the help of advisers inside and outside your firm, can take an early view on whether or not it was your company's fault. But you can easily be facing the tough questions before you know for sure what the entire situation regarding fault is. You clearly need to put steps in place to find out more.

There may be, for example, closed-circuit video footage of the incident, which would be very useful. If you're asked the questions before you have put all the right steps in place, then say what you *plan* to do in order to find out.

It's important that you come across on behalf of your company as humane and caring, while at the same time demonstrating a responsible attitude. And you need to do this without causing any unnecessary problems for your own company or making any admissions that your insurers, lawyers or bosses would not want you to make at this stage.

You can be faced with a particularly difficult challenge if you conclude that the fault actually lies with your client. The adage "the customer is always right" can be a helpful underlying commercial philosophy, but it isn't always technically correct. This is something you may not want to suggest too early in a developing situation, which is why it's important to put steps in place to find out all the facts as soon as possible – and to include a reference to this in your early answers. There can be a time to indicate that something is the client's fault, but you want to be on firm ground before you say it – and to have the wording well worked out before you open your mouth! Remember, what is said is ultimately determined by how it's said, so when the time comes it is worth working out the phrasing carefully so as to convey the truth but simultaneously keep the client onside if possible.

2. Embrace the CARE formula

It is because of this multitude of challenges when something has gone badly wrong that you need to embrace the CARE formula – "Concern, Action, Reassurance, Example". You may not say everything contained within the formula in your first answer, as it could be too longwinded. However, you need to cover each of the points in the formula early in the conversation.

In this particular instance involving questions from Petra about the ailing George, you certainly need to get the four elements of the CARE formula across early on in the conversation. But even before that you do of course need to ask more about the details of George's state of health – for humanitarian reasons, to demonstrate concern, and to build up a picture of how serious the situation is that you're facing.

Here are the kinds of things you can include while utilizing the CARE formula in this situation:

Concern: "I'm really sorry to hear about George's condition. Please give him our best wishes for a speedy recovery and keep us informed about his progress. I know George plays a critical role in your company's day-to-day operations, so I hope you can work out a way to keep things going effectively without him for the time being."

Action: "At the moment I can't give you an answer to your question as we are getting together all the details. And we need to take advice on what needs to be done in relation to George and your company's situation. I will get back to you as soon as our company has all the information we need, has received advice and decided what we can do in relation to George and to your company. And I will call you in three hours whatever we've achieved in order to give you an update.

We will of course seek to learn any lessons from this most unfortunate incident and make sure we apply them to the next two exercises in the series and to any others. I'll get our health and safety officer to look into this matter straight away. I will make sure he has access to the notes made by Cyril and David in the accident record book at the time and that he gets the witness statements that were gathered at the scene. We will make sure we notify any authorities who need to be told and keep them in the picture."

Reassurance: "As our job is to help ensure our clients act in accordance with the highest possible health and safety standards, we naturally take every step we can to ensure we act in the same way ourselves. As a result, situations like this are very rare."

Example: "In our twelve-year history, as far as I know, we have only had one other incident involving serious injury in one of our training sessions. This was seven years ago. In that case we did everything we could to ensure we acted in the proper way and learned the lessons involved. The client is still with us and we've done many more health and safety exercises with them that have all worked out very well and very safely."

So what has this kind of answer achieved?

It has:

- Followed the rule about talking to the heart before the head, so that an emotional connection is made with the client before dealing with the factual side of the situation.

- Taken a compassionate approach towards George and demonstrated a responsible approach towards the client.

- Backed up the concern with stated actions, so it's not just a matter of saying the right thing alone. These actions concern both the incident itself and the situation in the future.

- Explained why the questions about blame and compensation can't be answered immediately but provided an undertaking that they will be dealt with and when this will happen.

- Indicated that the right thing will be done with other bodies involved concerning health and safety.

- Given a reason why the client should be reassured about the situation with a view to the further planned exercises and beyond.

- Put the accident in a wider context by indicating how rare it is.

- Painted a picture in the client's mind about how another client stayed with the company after something similar happened – thereby seeking to maximize the prospects for this client staying on the books of the company.

- Delivered some positive messages from a difficult position.

- Taken a legally responsible approach without letting the threat of legal action get in the way of coming across with compassion and responsibility.

Keeping your clients on board through your great answers

As customer relationships are at the heart of all successful businesses, it's hard to overestimate the importance of getting it right in your conversations with clients.

You have an effective commercial responsibility and a powerful business incentive to answer tough questions from your clients as well as you possibly can. Your answers can ultimately play a major part in how you're seen as performing, and how your company is seen as performing – by your clients and by others.

In the challenging moments, you can seek to focus the answers you give to tough client questions to protect the business relationship as best you can. In the good times, you can use the tough questions to strengthen and grow the business relationship – and to lead both parties towards a deeper trusted advisor relationship and the greater success and prosperity that can go with it.

Chapter 13

GREAT ANSWERS IN THOSE NERVE-WRACKING JOB INTERVIEWS

Job interviews are not just about asking questions to get relevant facts out of you. The more challenging ones are designed to go way beyond that – and to find out what happens when you are subjected to pressure.

In some cases, such as those where the successful applicant will have to make rapid, difficult decisions, there is a logical strategy behind hurling those nerve-wracking pressure questions at you. In other situations, the questions are designed to see what uncomfortable truths you might blurt out about yourself under duress.

Whatever the motives of a selection panel, you need to go into job interviews ready to stand up to potentially unsettling questions – and to use The First Golden Formula to convey positive messages and thereby use them to your advantage. This applies to interviews at entry-level positions for first-time job seekers through to senior leadership positions. This chapter will look at giving great answers to tough job interview questions across all levels.

Find out all you can in advance

A lot of job applicants flunk the interview test before they walk through the door to shake hands with the panel. This is because they haven't found out as much as they should before they meet the selectors and haven't worked out in advance what they should be saying as a result. Your potential employers have invested some time in checking you out. So do the same with them.

The Internet makes much of this research very easy, but don't let that stop you pursuing other sources as well. If you can get an insider or two to tell you what the company really needs, and to brief you on the internal politics, then so much the better. Make sure you trawl the organization's website. Read the blog posts. Check out the online press releases. Look at who is who in the hierarchy. Examine any case study success stories.

Google the organization so you're not just subjected to the image they want to project to cyberspace. Find out the hot issues in the industry, if you don't already know.

Remember those two circles representing your agenda and their agenda, and find the overlapping zone between their interests and yours. They must already think there is some overlap or they wouldn't have invited you for interview. So make sure you reinforce their view on this.

Discover the challenges of their customers

Cast your research net wider than just the organization itself, and find out the challenges that the industry and its customers face. Discovering their customers' problems can help you spot ways to point out how you can help the company do better.

If you know in advance what their pain points are, and also what they're having success with, this will help you know where their questions to you may come from – and what you should touch on in your answers to increase their desire to have you on board. Your advance intelligence gathering will also help you ask insightful questions to them rather than just obvious ones.

Think through why you should have the job

While you're working out what are the worst questions they can ask you, make sure you're ready for that most basic question of job interviewers: "Why do you deserve this position?"

Whether it's asked in this form or in all sorts of other ways, you need to have a well-thought-out response to wow them in reply.

But as you prepare for it, let's also turn things around.

Ask yourself this question: "Why do you – Company X – deserve to have me in this job?" Make sure you *only* ask yourself this question. Never put it to them in this way, of course.

The first person you need to convince that you should have the job is yourself. If you can do that – without being overconfident or arrogant – then you're well on your way towards convincing them.

Of course, ultimately you are looking for a win/win. You need to convince each other that you can make an employee–employer arrangement work for both.

Like the pathway to true love, forging a great employee–employer deal doesn't always run smoothly. The answers you give during the job interview are crucial to whether or not there will be a deal. And if you choose to ask them questions – which you should – then your questions, as well as their answers, can also be crucial.

What's your deeper purpose for wanting this job?

While we are focusing on these matters, also take the trouble to ask yourself: "Why do I actually want this job?" Go beyond thoughts like "I have to pay the bills". If you can identify a deeper purpose, then you're well on the way to convincing both yourself and those on the other side of the table that the job should be yours. If, for example, you're applying for a job at a school or university, and you see it as one of your life purposes to enlighten the younger generation in your area of expertise, then you come across as a better candidate.

Despite the pressure, they usually want you to succeed

Members of selection panels have a strong incentive to get it right. If they succeed in this task, it reflects well on them. Their colleagues and their bosses will be delighted. And having the right people in the right positions is destined to make their life and everyone's life in the company all the better.

So the selectors ultimately should want to come up with an impressive winner. And their starting point with each new applicant who appears before them is likely to be that they want them to do well. But if, as the interview continues, they start to suspect that you may not be what the company needs, then they will feel obliged to test out that suspicion with tougher questions. You have to help convince them that you're the right fit for each other.

Candidates for first jobs in particular are often notoriously timid and don't have enough to say. Mere "Yes", "No" and "Don't know" answers are generally not that helpful to the panel or to you. Panel members have to be impressed – and to feel as though they have got to know you well enough that they can confidently say: "This person shines out as if they will be great in the post." Seeing how you react under pressure can help them feel as though they know you better. It also enables them to witness how you might be when in the position and things get rough. So don't take questions designed to pressure you as a personal affront. They're an opportunity to show that you can keep calm under pressure and have something significant to say.

So, doing well when answering their questions is often a matter of saying a bit more – providing it's a bit more of the right stuff. This is why you need to make sure you have your own agenda with your own messages and impressive things worked out in advance to drop into the conversation.

Projecting the right attitude

A successful company needs to have people who are both competent to do the work and have the right attitude so they are in harmony with the aims of the organization. But if they ever have to choose between these two, then logic dictates that it's the right attitude that's the more important for the overall health of the company. The thinking behind this is that you can have someone with the right attitude and, if necessary, help them become more competent. But if you have someone competent who has a negative, unhelpful, destructive attitude then this is a lot harder to fix. And unless the poor attitude is sorted, it will ultimately work against the interests of the company and have a downward effect on overall morale.

Attitude is critical for first-time job seekers

A first-time seeker of a full-time job by definition won't have a significant track record of competence to point to. But however little experience you've had, you can still demonstrate the right attitude. Exactly what this right attitude is varies from company to company. But it would most typically be positive, keen to learn, happy to work as a co-operative member of a team and enthusiastic about helping the company and its customers get to a higher level. The right attitude shouldn't mean accepting everything the company says and does totally without question. At the extreme end, this can lead to an Enron-style scandal, where too many people in the infamous American energy corporation unquestioningly went along with poor and unethical practices to hide debt and truth, which ultimately led to the company going out of business.

Notwithstanding this, the American motivational speaker Zig Ziglar had a point when he declared: "Your attitude, not your aptitude, will determine your altitude." So when you're thinking about the kind of impression you want to convey, include messages focusing on your attitude as well as your competence. And of course, you want to be able to come down that "Ladder of Abstraction" to back them up. If you are just starting on the career ladder, you can draw on experiences that you had at school, college or university, in a sports team, through work experience, charity or voluntary work or in a part-time job in order to come up with the right examples.

So having discussed what's required generally for a successful job interview outcome, let's look at some specific tough questions and potential answers.

Preparing for questions at a new full-time job interview

Let's imagine you are after a new full-time job but have no formal qualifications. You are very fond of animals and are devoted to your two hairy English sheep dogs, so you're keen to find a job that in some way involves pets.

You find an advertisement online for a "dog grooming assistant stylist" at a chain of stores that supplies pets and looks after their needs. The dog grooming takes place in a salon inside a store that's close to where you live. It's one of many grooming salons inside their expanding array of shops, so if you get work in one you figure you may well be able to transfer to a more responsible position in another shop at some point.

After having a good look at the company's website and making a point of visiting the local branch, you complete the online application form. You notice that many of the questions relate specifically to your attitude to work, to animals and looking after customers, including difficult ones. There are questions about whether you get satisfaction from doing a good job, whether you feel impatient with obnoxious people, and whether in a business like theirs you think the welfare of pets should be the highest priority. Apart from giving what should be the obvious online answers to such questions, the type of questions asked on an application form can give you helpful things to think about in terms of what they might want to explore in a job interview.

Fortunately for you, the form says that having a dog grooming or pet care-related qualification is not essential – though it would be beneficial. But while you don't have such a qualification, you do spot on the website that the company purports to offer fantastic learning and development opportunities. So you can reasonably surmise that if they take you on, they might actually help you get a qualification. This is certainly a good thing to ask about at an interview.

You speak to a contact you met through dog obedience school, who used to work at one of the company's dog grooming salons. Amongst the things he told you was that the biggest challenge in working there is to quieten and relax uptight dogs who don't want to be groomed – especially when they get so distraught that it puts other dogs on edge. This is a useful tip, as one of your skills – honed with your own dogs and through work experience at the local vets – is rapidly calming distressed animals.

Preparing your great interview answers

Remembering the AMEN preparation formula, let's go through what you need to do to ready yourself for the interview – and be poised to capitalize on any tough questions.

Audience: Your audience will be the grooming manager inside the local branch, with whom the successful applicant will be working. So they will want someone they can get on with and who will follow their instructions. You could assume that you might also be questioned by other colleagues, including the overall manager of the store. You notice on the website that it says that the overwhelming majority of those who work in the company are pet owners. This means that the employees you meet at the shop are highly likely to be pet owners themselves and therefore will have something in common with you. Asking about their pets or their favourite animals in the store could be worth doing at an appropriate point.

Message: Your headline message needs to capitalize on your limited experience and your love of dogs. Given that the website says looking after your own dogs doesn't count as professional experience, you need to make sure you don't put excessive emphasis on your experience with your own dogs. But it is still nonetheless worth dropping into the interview at certain points.

So, your headline message could be something like:

"My love of animals and experience with lots of dogs, including those I dealt with while on work experience with my local vet, makes me well equipped to help you run this dog grooming salon fantastically well."

Your other messages could include:

"I am keen to build on my existing dog-related skills quickly to help the team, the customers and their pets.

I'm especially good at calming dogs when they're stressed, which should be useful in an environment where there are a lot of dogs who can potentially upset each other."

Examples: To back up your headline message you can draw on specific examples of things that happened during your work experience with the vet. You could make mention of a reference the vet has written for you, which says you have a great affinity with dogs.

Negatives: You make a list of the negative questions they could ask you, and start thinking about how you can be ready to turn them to your advantage.

These questions include several that are very specific to your situation, such as: "Isn't it going to be difficult for you working here as you haven't done dog grooming as a full-time job before?"

There are also a number of questions that are typically thrown at applicants, which you want to be ready for – such as:

- How do you react to criticism? (This can be designed to elicit your attitude to authority and to your own improvement.)

- What are your long-term career plans? (This is a question that many people find difficult. Showing some longer-term ambition within their industry and framed in the interests of the company can be a real plus.)

- What is your biggest weakness? (This is always one to be prepared for, as you need to show some modesty without setting a trap for yourself.)

So let's take a look at how the ABCDE formula can be applied to a couple of these, starting with:

Isn't it going to be difficult for you working here as you haven't done dog grooming as a full-time job before?

Answer: "As I'm very interested in dog behaviour, I'm sure I would find working here fascinating."

Bridge: "What I'm particularly keen on doing to help out with is…"

Content of key message: "…calming dogs when they're stressed. This is something I have become good at – and which they found really useful at my local vet's when I was doing work experience in an environment where there were lots of dogs who can potentially upset each other."

Dangle: "For example, at the vet's…"

Example: "…there was one red setter who needed frequent treatment and who used to get distraught and upset the other dogs whenever he came in. He would bark crazily and run around frantically in small circles. I started asking the owner to give the dog a treat to settle him as soon as he arrived. Then I stroked the setter and spoke soothingly to him in the way I do with my own dogs when they get stressed. After a while the setter would become so relaxed and comfortable that he didn't actually notice when the owner left. And when it came to being washed he actually seemed to enjoy the experience."

What's your biggest weakness?

Saying you don't have a weakness is never an option!

You should always have something prepared that is slightly against yourself, but ultimately something that could either be seen also as a kind of strength or that could work to the advantage of the employer – such as: "Sometimes I get too obsessive about punctuality and care too much about turning up on time for things."

So perhaps in the context of the pet company, which declares that it seriously cares about the welfare of animals, your response could be something like:

Answer: "I get upset when anyone is cruel to a pet. I try not to show it too much."

Bridge: "But…"

Content of key message: "…I'd be keen to learn how to handle things ethically and properly if anyone was cruel to a pet in the shop – or if they indicated they were cruel to an animal at their home. So given the company's admirable policy on concern over animal welfare, I'd be interested to know if there are any guidelines on what to do about anyone who behaves badly towards a pet."

This takes the conversation onto much better ground for you – away from your weaknesses and onto an issue of importance for the company and one where they may be able to help you help them.

Dealing with pressure questions in interviews for senior posts

So let's jump ahead to interviews later in careers, when getting a senior position is a possibility.

In these cases your record in work – and how you present it – is crucial to your success. So it's important to be able to draw successfully on your experience, especially recent experience, to springboard yourself to a higher plane.

Let's suppose you have been doing remarkably well in the position as head of the Learning and Development Department at a company that runs highly successful telephone call centres. You've been at the forefront of implementing a policy to give the people who answer the phones at the call centres particularly high levels of training. You've been bringing in experts to run courses for them on dealing with different personality types, and to draw up profiles of certain types of customers so that the staff can quickly tell during a phone call the kind of person with whom they are dealing – and serve them so much more effectively as a result.

You have also been taking part in a business leaders group for those executives aspiring to work at the top of companies, so you've been exposed to experts who have been helping you and other members to develop your leadership skills. This has led you to get a very successful chief executive to mentor you, so you're better equipped to take on a higher-level position.

You apply to become the chief executive of a new, relatively small call centre company with big plans to specialize in handling phone calls for up-market companies which provide high-quality goods and services. Your application indicates that you believe the prospects of success for the new company could be strengthened if they provide exceptionally high levels of training for their call centre staff, as your current company has been doing under your guidance. This is enough to tempt the board of the new company to grant you an interview. But there is one particular tough question you know you need to be ready for when seeking to leap to become a chief executive for the first time:

How can you possibly be chief executive of our company when you haven't held a position at this level before?
You prepare the following to seek to capitalize on it with a variation of the ABCDE formula, which numbers points and gives examples where necessary as you make each point.

Answer: "Everyone who gets to be a chief executive has to make the jump up at some stage."

Bridge: "There are three important factors that equip me to make the jump for this role with your company."

Content of key message with examples: "The first is that I've been preparing myself for this kind of position over the past five years by being part of a business leaders group, which specifically trains members in the kind of skills they need to step up to being chief executive. As a result, I've had the benefit of training with and learning from some of the country's most prominent leadership experts, who have given our group advanced preparation for becoming CEO. This has covered a range of leadership issues, from formulating and implementing the overall vision through to team building and even, thinking a long way ahead, succession planning.

The second factor is that through the leaders group I've ended up acquiring a mentor who is a highly experienced and success-ful chief executive, and who over the past year has been prepar-ing me to take on a top job and showing me how he makes decisions and formulates and implements his plans for his company.

The third factor is that I've been putting this learning into action already in leading my department, which is responsible for training large numbers of staff and winning a series of top industry awards. So I can draw on this departmental leadership experience for the role of chief executive. Under my leadership of our department it has been recognized for taking call centre staff to unprecedented standards. This has been the backbone of our company's overall success and the rise in its share price over the past year by 43%. So I've already been playing an important leadership role in enabling a company serving up-market clients in the call centre industry to build its business base. My experience in leading the way in providing cutting-edge training for call centre staff will help put your company in a strong position to win the clients it needs to thrive in a very competitive marketplace. We need to lead your new company in a way that makes it a first choice call centre provider for clients who want their customers to get a top-level experience every time they make a phone call. My leadership experience and all the preparations I've been making to be a chief execu-tive can help you achieve that."

Do be aware that when you plan out an answer with numbered points it can be impressive, as it shows that you have thought through your position in advance. The danger to watch out for with numbered points is if you momentarily forget a point, which shows up when you suddenly can't recall what to say to match a number. So if you do plan the occasional answer with numbered points, you will want to practice it well and possibly, as a safety net, have a tiny, easy-to-read note as an almost invisible memory prompt somewhere which you can glance at if necessary.

Prepare for all those predictable job interview questions

By looking at all these kinds of specific challenging job interview questions, you can see how important it is – when the future of your career is at stake – to do prior planning on key answers rather than attempt to come up with something on the spot. When you focus your mind on a specific job interview situation, you can see that many tough job questions are quite predictable. All you need to do to work out many of them is put yourself in the mind of the interviewers who are seeking to test you out with a bit of pressure and plan your response in advance.

So whatever level the prospective job is at, it's worth putting in the time and effort in advance of the interview to make sure you're equipped with the kind of pre-prepared answers that will enable you to sail through the experience – and maybe even take you to the very top.

Chapter 14

GREAT ANSWERS FOR YOUR BOSS

The bossiest of bad bossy bosses get a negative rap in popular culture.

This especially applies to those real-life hard-to-please business tycoons on the so-called reality television show *The Apprentice* – played on the small screen by Donald Trump and Alan Sugar – who spend their time in the United States and the United Kingdom respectively asking contestants why their money-making plans went wrong before telling them: "You're fired!"

It similarly applies to the outrageously demanding Miranda Priestly – played on the big screen by Meryl Streep in *The Devil Wears Prada* – and supposedly modelled on a real-life fashion boss.

Scarier still, but in a different way, is the boss in the television show *The Office* – in versions on both sides of the Atlantic – who is particularly spooky when he's overly pushy, overly friendly and overly insensitive at the same time.

Whether bosses come across as monsters, control freaks, micro-managers, jerks or bumbling fools – or as enlightened, intelligent, well-rounded, caring, loveable creatures (yes, this happens sometimes in real life!) – most of them have at least one thing in common. They ask difficult, awkward and sometimes seemingly impossible questions:

> *"Why did this go wrong?"*
> *"Wasn't this entirely your fault?"*
> *"Are you looking for a new job?"*
> *"Shouldn't you start looking for a new job?"*
> *"How do you rate my performance as a manager?"*
> *"Will you take on this project that no one else is prepared to touch?"*

Whether or not your boss, past or present, is anything like the ones identified so far, they tend to ask challenging questions with an insider's knowledge of where the bodies lie. Even really fantastic bosses can ask questions as tough as those that Hercule Poirot or Columbo might ask. It's part of what bosses are paid to do.

There are all sorts of strategies for handling difficult bosses – from getting a mentor in the organization who is above your immediate boss in the pecking order, to keeping a diary about their unreasonable demands and putting it in the right hands. In this chapter we will naturally focus on how you answer their challenging questions. If this is done well it can have a big effect on the wider way you are perceived, the way you are treated and the way you can empower yourself to succeed.

We will also be looking at when things go wrong and your boss is asking questions based on the perception – misguided or accurate – that it's your fault.

But before that we will look at hopefully calmer routine planning and review conversations where you can use your pre-thought-out answers to challenging questions to get on the front foot and propel things in a positive direction. We'll also look at some of those tricky questions identified above that can be especially awkward when they come from someone who has immediate power over you.

Use your boss's questions to "manage upwards"

There is a simple definition of a boss as one who has the job of telling others what to do. But there is a great modern concept that can potentially level out the power imbalance implied by this definition. It's called "managing upwards", and relates to how you can help your boss to help you – and hopefully others and the wider organizational interest at the same time.

The key to answering the boss's questions and simultaneously managing upwards is to go into those conversations about preparing for the future and reviewing your development with a positive plan of your own. This can be a plan for how you would like to develop within the organization and involve things which your boss can do to help, such as signing off your participation on certain courses to build your skill base or bringing in a coach to help you progress.

Having your own constructive agenda for such conversations could simply involve coming up with a plan for how you think a particular project should be undertaken, or how a project already on the agenda could best be tackled. It doesn't have to be a totally comprehensive plan – it could just be one or more positive ideas on how you and/or others can contribute to and build on existing plans. It's particularly good to have this worked out when going into situations such as a staff appraisal or a monthly review with your boss. Here's an example.

I had a situation while a lecturer at a university where I was greatly enjoying the work, but wanting to simultaneously take up more training and professional-speaking opportunities outside the institution. Because of the scheduled times with my students, I turned down an invitation to run a few days' worth of media training courses for diplomats in Chile, which I would have loved to do. It would have been great for my own development (and hopefully for the diplomats too!). I then felt bad about that missed opportunity. So when soon afterwards I was asked to run another short series of media training courses for diplomats in Japan, where I was extremely keen to go, I took a chance and asked the boss if it were possible to get a part-time lecturer in to cover the days I would be in Tokyo and Osaka. Breathtakingly he agreed in an instant, saying how good it would be for the university to have someone picking up that kind of experience overseas. I then kicked myself even harder over having missed the earlier opportunity to work in Santiago!

Having learned from that, when my staff appraisal was coming up with another boss, I was inspired to go into the session with plans to do a bit more work outside the university, which a little time-tabling flexibility and outside back-up would enable. So I included this in part of the answers to those standard questions about how you see yourself developing over the next few years. Again the response was a remarkably speedy "Yes", and an acknowledgement that this would both be good and look good for the university. As the university was seeking to attract more international students and also to build its own media training courses, there were indeed win/win outcomes to be had. But they only worked out because the crucial part of the appraisal discussion had been planned in advance.

Utilize critical questions to springboard onto what you require

Once you have your own agenda for that conversation with the boss, the key to getting onto it is usually the ABCDE formula. You can do this in response to positive questions about where you would like to be in the future. But you can also do the same with those questions that involve criticism of your performance.

There is a saying that can be helpful in these performance-related conversations with the boss: "All feedback is good feedback." With this in mind you can use any negatives concerning your performance to work with your boss to do something positive for yourself and your organization.

Let's suppose you struggle with drawing up spreadsheets and making presentation slides on your computer. This is because you have just picked things up along the way and have never been formally shown how to use them properly. So you put on your agenda a proposal for the company to send you on courses to master these skills. This makes the following apparently negative question a gift:

> "Do you agree that your performance is being held back by your weakness in handling technology?"

So here is how you can deploy the ABCDE formula to head onto the territory that you need to get to.

Answer: "There is some truth in that."

Bridge: "And I'm really keen to overcome this so I can be more productive and quicker in my work."

Content: "At times I struggle with some programmes on the computer because I've never been shown how to do them step by step, and I've only picked up what I do know on the run."

Dangle: "So I've been thinking about this and the best thing to do would be…"

Example: "…for me to go on two open courses that are coming up – one on spreadsheets and one on presentation slides. This would make a big difference to me being able to impressively set out work to present to our clients and to have it ready more quickly."

So, having your own agenda, you have used ABCDE to gravitate onto it at the right moment. Once there, you have taken the opportunity to ensure that your answers are focused – not just on your own interests, but on the overlapping "What's In It For Me?" factor for your boss and your organization as well.

When things go wrong, establish your position before the questions start

When something you've been involved with has gone wrong and you believe you will be questioned as a "suspect" or, worse still, as the "guilty party" there is one thing you have to do very early. If possible, work out whether or not you believe you are at fault. If necessary, hold a quick commission of inquiry against yourself so you know where you stand in relation to the allegations.

If the situation is a grey area, seek to identify what you did wrong and what you did right – and the same for any others involved. If it's complicated, then there's all the more reason to figure out where you and any others stand in relation to what has gone wrong before you open your mouth.

Whether the situation concerning who is at fault is obvious or fuzzy, it's much safer for you to go into the conversation with a clear idea of the rights and wrongs of the situation before the questions start. If it's not your fault, work out whether the situation is nonetheless your responsibility. Make sure you identify to yourself in advance whether there are any specific things that you or any others should have done to have prevented the problem. And with a view to making things better in the future, look at what needs to be done now about the current situation as well as what ought to be done differently in future to avoid similar problems recurring.

Let's consider a situation where you are – in the first instance – "in the wrong" and then – in the second instance – "in the right". One of the reasons why you need to establish your position in relation to the allegation ahead of the conversation is that it makes a difference to which of the golden formulae you use.

Responding to the boss when you are at fault

Suppose you are a website manager who has recently been taken on board by your new company because it wants to look more impressive in cyberspace. With approval from the board, you commission a new corporate video to go on the website. Under your guidance, a production company that's already on the books as a supplier produces a great video which meets with general acclaim. As the newest team member you're not familiar with your company's routine procedures governing how projects are financially signed off. No one gave you a briefing on this, and you didn't specifically ask. When the invoice comes from the production company, it's 20% higher than what the Finance Department says was budgeted for. No one had discussed the budget side with you, and you were under the impression that the Finance Department had a standard pricing arrangement with the production company about costs. Unfortunately, it didn't.

Having learnt this, you now realize that you should have sought a specific quotation and obtained the Finance Department's acceptance of it. Your boss has scheduled a meeting with you, where you will need to answer the question: "How did you manage to allow spending on the video project to go 20% over budget?"

You do a quick review before the meeting, and decide that while it may not have precisely been your fault, it probably was ultimately your responsibility.

It would have been good if someone in finance had given you a briefing on how the sign-off system worked, but as this wasn't forthcoming you realize you should have been more pro-active in overseeing the budgetary side of the project. You therefore decide that making an apology is the honourable thing to do.

Because something has gone wrong, and your boss and others are upset about it, you need The Second Golden Formula, where you touch on the emotional side at the start of the conversation. You therefore put the apology at the front of your answer, to try to take the sting out of the situation from the start. So, your answer based on the CARE formula looks like this.

Concern: "I'm sorry the video project has gone over the approved budget; I was unaware of the details of how the financial sign-off works here. Even though no one volunteered to brief me, I realize that it was ultimately my responsibility to find out how the system works."

Action: "I will make sure I get a briefing from the Finance Department immediately, so I know exactly what to do in future."

Reassurance: "I am aware of how important it is that spending is properly controlled, so I want to be in a position to make sure it works out well with the next videos – which I've been asked to work on straight away."

Example: "The board members have been so delighted with the quality of the video, and are so confident it will bring in new clients, that the chief executive told me last week he wants me to oversee the production of more videos for the website in the same style and with the same supplier. So I'll make sure the finance procedures are followed rigorously with each of these."

Responding to the boss when you think you're innocent

Now let's look at the same scenario, but happily assume that you had wisely taken the initiative of first seeing one of the finance officers about the budgetary sign-off. He said he would sort everything on the budgetary side and sent you an email to this effect. So when the invoice comes in at 20% higher than expected, you are totally in the clear.

In this instance you can use something closer to the ABCDE formula. But as your boss is upset about the situation, it would be wise to still touch on the "Concern" element from the CARE formula at the start of your answer. So here is how this slight variation on the ABCDE formula could work effectively.

Answer: "I'm concerned and surprised that there's any problem with the invoice. The finance officer I dealt with specifically approved the expenditure and sent me an email to say it was all being sorted."

Bridge: "But to make sure we prevent a recurrence of this..."

Content of key message: "...it would be good if I had a talk with the Finance Director later today about how best to handle budgetary sign-offs to ensure we do everything possible to avoid the problem recurring in the future."

Dangle: "For example…"

Example: "…with the company wanting more of these videos in the near future, as a way of boosting business, it's important we get the financial sign-off handled smoothly every time."

So in this instance you've hopefully connected with the boss emotionally in the right way at the start of your answer, as well as made it clear that you had done the right thing and properly checked out the situation with the Finance Department.

You have effectively bridged onto your key message that you take the financial side of things seriously and will seek to stop the problem occurring again. You have then moved onto a positive example, and underlined the point that the video you commissioned was popular and is seen as likely to increase business. And you have concluded with a happy prospect of getting financial sign-off every time in the future.

A look at other tricky boss questions

Let's look at a couple of other questions from the boss mentioned earlier that might prove tricky. Of course there's no end to the questions that can come up, but what's important is to get used to using the methods in the most effective way. So let's go through the AMEN preparation framework for a couple of them.

How would you rate my performance as a manager?
This is indeed a bit on the tricky side. It's one thing for your boss to be rating your performance, but a touch awkward for it to be the other way around.

As ever, it might be worth asking a few questions and saying you'll give it a bit of thought before you actually deliver the verdict. Ideally you will want to discover the motive for the question. Is it a simple case of wanting a genuine constructive critique with a view to improvement? Is it based on a touch of insecurity – so it's more about fishing for compliments? Or has someone higher up the chain made a critical comment about how the boss manages those reporting to them, meaning that your answer could potentially be used as ammunition in a battle?

For the purposes of the exercise, let's work on the assumption that it's a straightforward request for an objective assessment in order to help the boss get to a higher level of performance. And we will assume that the boss has a range of good and bad points that you could refer to. Even though you would want to be professionally objective, there is also an opportunity for you to reasonably help yourself and the team by reinforcing the boss's good points and picking on a negative one where you and others might benefit from an improvement. (It may be wise and diplomatic to keep it to just one negative!) In this case you might want to adopt a variation of The First Golden Formula, which is a bit like a sandwich with two very tasty fresh slices of bread but an unpleasant filling.

So, you can start on a positive point that would be good to reinforce. This is represented by the top slice of bread. You then bridge onto the negative point, represented by the unpleasant filling. However, being constructive, you should couple it with a way of showing how the boss could improve on this point. So you can dangle an example of what the boss could do to turn a negative into a positive. However, that may well not be the safest place to conclude. So you would then have a second bridge to move onto the second slice of tasty fresh bread. In this way you are effectively ending on a positive to leave the boss and yourself with a nice taste in your mouths!

Depending on your relationship with your boss and your boss's character, you can make a fine judgement call about how much detail if any you want to get in. Remembering the different personality types we examined at the end of Part One, it's quite likely that your boss is a "Director" personality. As such, he will want you to stick to your point and will not want a lot of detail. However, Directors do tend to like enough detail to underpin credibility. And as you know, it is generally good to back up a message by going down that "Ladder of Abstraction" and painting a picture with a specific example. If you were going to do this in order to give the boss an example of where his management style could be improved, use your thinking time carefully to pick a situation that isn't going to be upsetting, controversial or counterproductive for you. As a helpful colleague you only want to be telling exact truths, but it would be wise to select any illustration with great care.

So let's take a look at one more particularly tricky question from our list:

Will you take on this project that no one else is prepared to touch?

In truth, if your boss is cunning he won't include the reference to others not wanting to take on the project. But you would probably know if the project concerned wasn't the most popular task going.

Of course, handled in the right way, taking on a project no one else wants to go near and doing it well could have all kinds of benefits. But for the purposes of the exercise, let's assume you are feeling pressured by your existing workload and that it would be irresponsible for you to take on this extra difficult project as the standard of your work would be bound to drop. So you need to get this across in order to ensure that your answer hits the "What's In It For Me?" factor for your boss and the company. This could involve painting a verbal picture of how other clients would suffer and be unhappy if you took on this additional project. This may be a case where an illustration could work – telling how one client might suffer if you were to be made responsible for an extra job that was more than you had time to do properly.

Choosing an example of a client close to the boss's heart might be good, and finding a way to show that the client would be angry if he felt in any way neglected by your company. If it were in line with the truth, you might even want to suggest that the client could be inclined to take a complaint to a high level, which could have painful consequences for the organization in general and your boss in particular. At the same time, you need to ensure that you come across with a positive, enthusiastic attitude to your work. So if you could find an example of some other way that you would be prepared to help share the work burden and do something extra for the organization, then this could be a good example to end on.

Questions from the boss can be amongst the hardest of the questions you have to deal with in the workplace, because of the power that can be wielded over you.

Careful thinking in advance, thoughtful selection of examples and meticulous wording of replies all play a part in helping you get the results you're after. It's difficult territory, but if you play your cards well you can end up having far more power over your own work life and your own future than you may ever have imagined.

Chapter 15

GREAT ANSWERS IN PRESENTATIONS, AT EVENTS AND IN MEETINGS

You're on the platform giving the best talk you've ever done in your life. It's in front of the biggest, most important gathering of your career...

Your audience members are being swept away by your insights. They've been moved to the edge of tears and the edge of their seats by the emotion, energy and excitement of your personal stories. They've been doubling up with laughter over your punch-lines. They've been adjusting their views in response to the brilliant arguments and enlightening truths you've been unveiling.

You're doing what all those on speaking platforms should aspire to do. You're not just being a mere deliverer of information – you're being an enlightener. You're being an educator. And you're being an audience shifter. You're pointing your audience members where they need to head in future and giving them inspired guidance on how to get there.

And now they're being wowed by your conclusion that draws together every magnificent element you've touched on into an earth-shattering climax. The applause is thunderous. Everyone in the massive auditorium, except for one person, is on their feet cheering and demanding more.

Then it happens.

It's time for their questions and your answers. And when everyone else sits, that one person at the venue who didn't take part in the standing ovation gets to his feet. He moves slowly to the microphone. He hesitates nervously for a moment. He clears his throat with a determined, nasty, grating cough. Then he spits out the worst possible question.

It's that nightmare, killer question – the very question that you woke up in a cold sweat about at three o'clock in the morning, thinking: "I hope no one asks me that!"

Ideally, by this stage of your progress through this book you're so empowered about giving great answers to tough questions that you feel as though you can handle almost anything that's thrown at you.

But just in case you haven't quite yet reached that happy state for every possible surprise savage question, then read on...

Ensuring your presentation inspires those questions

There is an alternative nightmare scenario around question and answer (Q&A) sessions. And I bet you've witnessed this on at least a few occasions...

It's when the presentation comes to an end and the person delivering it, or the compere, says something like: "So now it's time for questions. Who has a question? ... Does anyone have any questions? ... Anyone? ... There must be someone with a question... Surely..."

There are all kinds of pitfalls when it comes to Q&A sessions during presentations, events and meetings. A badly set up or badly handled question period can ruin, undermine or render forgotten your splendid presentation that came before.

A big part of the challenge is that you don't just have to generate stimulating questions, you have to give answers that go beyond merely satisfying the question asker. You have to come up with answers that ideally work for every other member of the audience as well.

With all those people watching and listening, if you don't receive any questions at the moment they're invited it can be as embarrassing as getting caught out being unable to make a great response to that venomous, killer question. If either of these things happen, you need to contemplate something harsh but true: It's your fault!

In the case of getting no questions, it probably means you haven't forewarned or inspired your audience properly. In the case of a tough question, where you have nothing useful to say it probably means you haven't prepared properly.

But the good news is that with effective preparation, planning and practice, both these embarrassing situations in front of audiences can be avoided.

Making the most of the Q&A session
A well-set-up and well-handled Q&A session adds value to the occasion. It allows you further opportunities to get your points

across and to take the audience further towards where they need to be taken.

This chapter will show you how to avoid the things that can potentially go wrong in Q&A sessions on big occasions with an audience – and how to maximize your chances of success.

In the first part, we'll look at situations where you're doing a pre-prepared talk – or at least part of your pre-prepared talk – before the questions start. This is a situation where you have a big chance to influence potential questioners through what you say to them before the time for questions is declared.

Later we will examine situations, such as at events or meetings, where you're in the spotlight just for the questions alone, without the opportunity of doing a setup talk at the start. This could be when you're on a panel at an event or where you alone are asked questions as part of a client meeting or an internal planning or board meeting.

Whatever the situation, you'll know from what you've read so far that preparation can play a big part in your success.

Let's start with a situation involving a presentation where questions and answers are going to play a significant part.

This is where getting things right in what you say before the first question is uttered helps get you in the best possible place to generate the right sort of questions at the right time and deal with them in the right way. This is also the part which helps prevent the traumatic situation of opening the question session and getting that embarrassing non-acceptance of your invitation – leaving you to beg for contributions or abandon the session. We don't want that to happen to you!

Ensuring your audience is inspired to ask

When you've been talking in the lead-up to a Q&A session and it produces no immediate questions, this suggests that perhaps you've been too dull, too uninspiring or said too little – or alternatively that you've said too much and left nothing more that people want to hear about. You have to inspire them to ask great questions. You don't do that by telling them absolutely everything in exhaustive detail during your presentation, leaving nothing more for them to ask.

In order to get it right, we can draw on the ancient Greek wisdom of Socrates on education – as a key purpose of your talk is, in some ways, to educate. Socrates proclaimed that education is about lighting a fire, not filling a vessel. Your talk needs to provide the sparks to set alight ideas for stimulating questions.

But people won't usually ask questions if they haven't had the chance to think about them. Audience members need enough time to frame thoughtful questions that they're confident enough to ask in front of everybody. So it's vital that you, or the person who introduces you, gives notice about the opportunity to ask questions.

There's a term we use in the broadcast media world called "signposting", where you indicate along the way what will be happening next. Radio stars are particularly keen on it, as they want to entice their audience to keep listening by continuously telling them what they'll be hearing later. They say things like: "And coming up in the programme is…" They'll especially do this if there is an audience phone-in session, because they know that they need to prompt listeners to call.

Just as throughout a highway network there's more than one "signpost" to an important place, ideally you will signpost the Q&A session several times in at least a couple of ways – thereby building expectations that a fantastic opportunity to pick your brain is lurking over the horizon. Apart from making an initial announcement about the Q&A session, when you touch on a particularly fascinating area of your subject you can further prompt your audience by saying "when it's time for questions, you might want to ask more about this". You need to have enough signposts and enough captivating material so that at least some audience members will be salivating at the prospect of asking you something.

While you're promoting the opportunity to ask questions, it's also the ideal time to lay down some valuable guidelines. Misguided audience members sometimes see the Q&A session as an opportunity to make a speech of their own. This isn't appropriate or helpful. You can seek to head off this possibility before it starts with a little request-cum-rule, like: "Please make sure that what you contribute to the Q&A session is actually a question."

Also, if there's a particular reason to stay away from any aspect of the subject then signal this beforehand. For example, if the head of your company is speaking after you then you might want to suggest that any questions on company policy be saved for your leader. Questioners, being human, won't always stick to "the rules" you lay down. But the good thing about mentioning the rules first is that it is then much easier to remind the miscreant questioner or speech maker that they're going against what you'd set out earlier – rather than introducing a rule on the spot and looking as though you've done it just to avoid their question.

With the Q&A session in mind, one thing to be aware of when crafting your talk to inspire questions is that audiences don't typically just want a whole lot of facts on the designated topic. They want your take on it. This can be provocative or controversial – though it doesn't have to be. But it certainly needs to be mighty interesting. If you get this right, your audience will be more inclined to want to ask you questions and get more out of you. Even if lunch is approaching, if you play it right everyone in the room will be prepared to override their hunger pangs and focus on the fantastic opportunity to squeeze another pearl of wisdom from you, providing you don't actually eat into their designated mealtime.

So, for the success of the questions and answers, what comes before them is as important as the Q&A session itself. Or, put more positively, as this book likes to do: There are things you can and should do to make sure that you get questions in the right way, to fuel the session.

Integrating your presentation and the Q&A session

When there's a Q&A session accompanying your talk, it's important to see the pre-prepared section of the presentation and the Q&A session as part of the same whole.

As you now know, answering questions is not just a chance to deliver facts. It's also an opportunity to convey a message or a series of messages. It is exactly the same with presentations.

So, look at the pre-prepared part of the presentation along with the Q&A session as a combined opportunity to get across your messages and shift your audience members in the direction they need to be shifted.

Putting the two elements together allows you to have more control over the Q&A part. And the key thing here is to take control of it. You are there to serve your audience, but taking control of the questions part in an enlightened way is done in their best interests as well as yours.

First, let's focus on the combined purpose of your presentation and the Q&A session. When I'm working with clients to boost their presentation skills, one of the key things is to get them to specifically identify the purpose of their talk. In order to assist them in this, I ask them to answer a vital question: "What is it you want your audience to be thinking or doing or feeling at the end?" Once the answer to this is established, then everything in the presentation should go towards achieving it.

So the outcome of the Q&A session should also be to move your audience further towards what you want them thinking, doing and feeling at the end. Viewed in this way, the Q&A session ceases to be perceived as a potentially troublesome part of the exercise that can sweep you off course. Instead, it helps you see the Q&A session as an opportunity to help achieve the real overall purpose that you have for that particular audience.

In order to achieve this, don't leave it to chance when and how questions will arise. Establish guidelines and expectations right at the start – for the audience's benefit as well as for yours.

Now before looking further at exactly how to do this, let's focus on different types of talks at conferences and seminars. There are many ways they can be classified. But if you look at it for a moment the way professional speakers do, there are two broad categories – the keynote and the workshop.

Questions during and after "the keynote"
The "keynote" category is typically for larger audiences – from a few dozen to hundreds or sometimes thousands. This is where the speaker talks with the primary aim being to inform and/or persuade. The expectation here is that the speaker will do all or most of the talking within the time slot. Questions are normally left to

the end or near the end. In this format, where the speaker has important things to expound, it usually makes sense to get everything out in the open so that the audience is then in a good position to ask questions, having already gained an understanding of the speaker's views on the topic.

Questions during the "workshop"

The "workshop" category is typically for smaller audiences – often less than twenty. The purpose of this is directed more at giving the participants the chance to try out putting the speaker's ideas and guidance into practice in order to build their skills in the subject area. The workshop tends to be more interactive throughout, and so questions are often allowed and encouraged at any point. Because the primary purpose is to develop skills, it makes sense for participants to ask a question whenever they feel the need so they're fully in the picture.

Set out the question guidelines early

Not every talk in the workplace fits entirely within these two categories. But they do provide a useful way to break up individual talks as far as the Q&A sessions are concerned. Whatever the category your presentation falls into, it's helpful for everyone if you set out the guidelines on questions near the start.

I advocate having a "roadmap" section in talks that outlines where things will be going in both keynotes and workshops. Typically this roadmap should be unveiled fairly close to the beginning, but not absolutely at the start. It's usually better to place it a few minutes in, after you have delivered a profound attention-grabbing opening. Audiences tend to like an early roadmap because, just as on a scenic bus tour, they want to know something about the destination you'll be taking them to and what the points of inter-est will be along the way. Then, when they get to each point, they feel reassured and excited that they're exactly where you said they would be. This also applies to the timing and any rules about ques-tions. In the roadmap section, tell them whether you would welcome questions at any point throughout or whether you would prefer them to keep their questions for a designated Q&A session – and if so, when that will be.

In a keynote it's especially important to endeavour to set out the guidelines before the first question is lobbed at you. Then you can rightfully say that you'll come to that point in the Q&A session – or that the point will be covered further into the talk. As your talk is hopefully carefully structured, you don't want to have to reorder it on the run just because of a random question. So you can acknowl-edge the question and say you'll answer it at the appropriate point. You can even ask the questioner to remind you in the Q&A session if they haven't received the information or opinion they want. Audi-ence members will generally be happy that you're sticking to what you said you would do. In this way you get to deal with questions at a point when you have built up that shared understanding of the topic with your audience, so everyone is in a better position to appreciate both a good question and your great answer.

As to the timing of questions in a keynote, my recommendation is normally to have the Q&A session near the end but not abso-lutely at the end. The advantage of this is that you – as the speaker – get to keep control of those vital last words at the close of your time on the platform, which guides your audience towards what you want them thinking, doing and feeling at this vital concluding moment. If you have the Q&A session at the very end, then your final point will finish on whatever topic you're asked about last. However insightful the final question is, it may not fit with what's best for you to conclude on for that audience on that topic.

So if you have the Q&A session a little before the end, it allows you to give your final answer and then move on to your pre-prepared conclusion. You may well make reference to one or more things that have come up in the questions as you adapt it in the moment. But by ending how you planned to end, you have the final say in how your talk closes – thereby maximizing the prospect of shifting the audience in the direction you want for them.

When it comes to the Q&A session, make a point that this is a big opportunity – as foreshadowed earlier. With a larger audience in particular, it's often best to ask people to raise their hand if they have a question – which avoids a bunch of questions being shouted at you at once and keeps you more in control.

As many people are reluctant to ask a question at the start of the Q&A session, it can be wise to have someone lined up to ask that first question. It may be someone who asked you a question privately earlier in the day, or someone you know is good at confidently asking pertinent questions. As a back-up, in case there are no immediate volunteers, you may also want to have a couple of questions in mind yourself that you can throw in by prefacing them with "I'm often asked…" or "Before I began someone asked…" and answer these questions. This will hopefully warm things up for other questions to flow.

In some places where there are loads of questions, there's a format where the organizers get three or four people to ask their questions in a row and then the answerer deals with each of them in a bunch. I abhor this, and am campaigning to outlaw it. I reckon it's generally not effective as it reduces the easy-to-follow pattern of a single question being followed by an immediate single answer. So I do suggest you use your influence to ensure you answer questions one at a time.

In a workshop, because it tends to be interactive throughout, I recommend that after an arresting start, you typically ask all the participants (or a sample of them): "What is it that you would like to know or to do better (or even better) by the end?" This equips you with a good idea of what each person who responds is most interested in – so it gives you an early indication of what questions they might ask. If you have the luxury of assistants helping you in the workshop, I suggest you ask them to write the topics raised on a flipchart or have them projected onto a screen where technology allows. If neither is possible, then make a brief note of the comments yourself. This will enable you to easily come back to these topics during the workshop and ensure that you satisfy everyone around the table. It also means that if you don't get enough questions at any point, then you can go back to what's been recorded and talk a little more on any of the topics listed.

Let the show proceed

Whether you're doing a keynote or a workshop, it's important to realize that at its best it is a kind of "show" – and the questions and answers can form an important part. As far as possible, you want the show to proceed smoothly – and if there's a hiccup, there's much to be said for the adage "the show must go on". In order to ensure this, careful planning and preparation is important – including the roadmap and the guidelines dealing with the questions and answers element. Effective preparation and delivery of these elements maximizes the chances of your show being a rip-snorting success.

Guidance on answers in meetings

When you're answering questions in client meetings, board meetings or other meetings, including "virtual town hall" live hook-ups through the Internet, the "show" element is typically not the same as at a presentation. These meetings are often fixed on getting the right outcomes and making the right decisions. So while you're still performing when responding to questions, your answers may not be as dramatic or performance-orientated as they can be when delivered as part of a presentation.

And unless you're chairing the meeting yourself, there's less likelihood that you'll be giving any kind of introductory talk before you answer questions. So you probably won't have the same possibility of setting out question guidelines as you do in your presentation, when the audience is in your hands before and during the Q&A session.

This means that your answers will be most effective if they're delivered as self-contained bite-sized chunks – not dependent on any prelude in order to be completely understood. So you need to be very aware that you may have to work a little harder to keep your audience in the picture as you give your answers – in order to ensure that you're maximizing your chances of connecting effectively with everyone at the meeting.

Questions at meetings can also come to you at any time, with less warning or predictability. So you need to have messages and illustrations at the ready to inject into your great answers, so that you're doing more than delivering straight information.

This allows you to kick that goal every time the ball comes your way.

Answers for your entire audience

Here's some guidance for your answers when dealing with questions in all situations where you have to consider the wider audience beyond the individual questioner at presentations, events and meetings. In each case it's vital to keep in mind that your answers have to be relevant to everyone involved – not just the question asker. You never want it to become a one-on-one conversation between you and the questioner, and allow others to feel like mere voyeurs. The challenge is to talk to the questioner in such a way that everything is relevant and engaging to everyone in the room and, where there's a live hook-up, electronically beyond.

This should be reflected in your eye contact. While listening to the question, it's right to focus just on the person asking it – and this will help ensure you listen as carefully as you should. But when it comes to your answer, make a point of allowing your eye contact to roam around the whole audience to ensure they know your answer is for them as well. When there's a virtual audience outside the room, look down the camera lens periodically to ensure your remote participants feel included.

There is a particular danger of exclusion if the question is a very specific one, inviting an answer on an obscure subject that potentially only the questioner is interested in. If this is the case, then you can promise to have a one-to-one conversation with the asker afterwards. But you should normally aim to capitalize on the question, however narrow, and make a response that will involve and captivate the wider audience. Your lifeline here is the "specific-to-general" approach. So if you're asked about something as narrow as business opportunities in sheep-related industries in the remote town of Gadooga in outback Australia, because the questioner is going on a visit there, this may not automatically be of interest to others in the audience – especially as Gadooga was once awarded the title of "Most Boring Town In Australia". So, in order to be useful and engaging for everyone, you could frame your reply in terms of sheep-related business opportunities across Australia – or possibly sheep-related business opportunities in remote towns around the world – by deftly moving from the micro to the macro.

You can use the specific-to-general technique to underpin an answer following the ABCDE formula. So very briefly answer or acknowledge the specific question, but then use the bridge to widen things. A bridging line could be "What will interest everybody here is..." or "To broaden the point then..." or "To give you an answer in a wider context..." The content of your message should be something that has relevance for the whole audience. Then, when you dangle an example, pick something from your treasure chest of case studies and stories that will appeal to all.

When you're in a situation where not everyone in the audience may have heard a question then it's good to repeat it, though don't repeat questions routinely unless poor acoustics or microphone problems make this necessary. Normally, if you don't understand the question, then immediately invite the asker to clarify it so your grasp of the question is clear.

But as you will have noticed, not all questions on big occasions are brilliantly worded. So if it's a sloppy or unclear question, you can take the opportunity to reframe it, saying something like: "I take it that what you're essentially asking is..." and proposing a pithier, tighter version of the question in your own words before answering it.

If the question is one of those rambling, multi-pronged ones, which is effectively a series of questions, then you're entitled to focus predominantly on the prong that suits you best – and that you judge will be of most interest to your audience. And if, due to the asker's incoherence, it will be too exhausting for everyone to ask a series of clarification questions, you might find it better to respond to a fragment of the question that you do understand. It can be a response like: "I'm sorry I can't quite grasp every detail of your question, but I would like to respond to your reference to X..." This can be a useful technique for any question that's too convoluted to follow. In the interests of keeping the show going, it can be best to use a part of the question you did grasp as a prompt to say something helpful on that aspect.

One thing to avoid doing too often is to praise the question. "That's a good question" has become a highly repetitive cliché. When the question is a tough one it can sound too deferential to the asker, as if you are grovelling before them. And praising the question is a particularly dangerous thing to do with a highly critical question. To illustrate my point, when I'm training people, I ask them to test out replying with "That's a good question" to an inquiry like: "Is it true that you've always been a liar, a cheat and a criminal and that you have a lot to hide from the police, the public and the tax department?" This normally cures them.

Another thing to avoid in most cases is saying "Have I answered your question?" at the end. Occasionally it may be appropriate, but in most cases it signals unnecessary uncertainty. Because you are the one who is answering the questions, you are in the position of authority. So unless there is particular reason to display uncertainty, it's better to confidently and profoundly say what you know to be true and say it in a way that projects confidence in its value. If the audience feels that you haven't answered, they will let you know!

Answering questions effectively in front of an audience isn't always easy or comfortable, but it can involve great opportunities to advance your career, your standing and the causes that you are pushing – and to take audiences to new levels of understanding in your areas of expertise. Audiences notice when you do it well – especially when the questions are tough. So with the right planning, preparation and practice, it's well worth embracing opportunities to get yourself out there in front of challenging Q&A sessions to enlighten, enthral and bedazzle with your great answers, not just for the individual questioners but for everyone.

Chapter 16

SHINING OUT THROUGH THE MEDIA AND AT PUBLIC GRILLINGS

Once upon a time there was a high-ranking politician who did a media interview that would haunt him for the rest of his career.

The haunting was for one reason – because he didn't answer the critical central question, even though he was asked it repeatedly…

The interviewer ended up asking the politician the same question more than a dozen times in a row.

Each time it was asked, the politician did not answer it directly.

The interviewer received praise and awards for his technique and persistence.

The politician did not come off so well.

The politician was ambitious to get to the very top. He wanted to be Prime Minister of Britain.

But he never made it.

There were a number of factors behind his failure to get there. One of them was the haunting interview.

The politician was called Michael Howard.

At the time of the interview in 1997, Mr Howard was seeking the leadership of his party in opposition as a springboard to gaining the prime ministership.

The interview focused on the time when Mr Howard had earlier been in government as the minister in charge of the prison service and other security matters. His title had been "Home Secretary".

The interview was conducted by the legendary go-for-the-jugular television presenter Jeremy Paxman, live on the British Broadcasting Corporation's *Newsnight* programme.

I draw attention to the Howard–Paxman interview when seeking to encourage clients to tackle tough questions head on – especially if they're reluctant to do this.

It shows what can happen if you don't answer a burning question without giving an excellent reason.

The interview focused on what happened after a series of highly publicized prisoner escapes, which was embarrassing for the government. The key question concerned whether Mr Howard had threatened to overrule the director-general of the prison service about a decision to suspend a prison governor after the escapes.

Asked by Jeremy Paxman if he'd threatened to overrule the director-general – which he was not technically supposed to do – Mr Howard started his replies with lines such as "I took advice on what I could and couldn't do…" and "I have accounted for my decision…" and "The important aspect of this…"

The points he made were significant, but they didn't directly answer the question, which is why Jeremy Paxman kept asking it.

You'll recall the term "bridge", which is that verbal device enabling you to move gracefully from one aspect of a topic to another in order to get your message across. And you'll remember that a bridge only works effectively when you properly deal with the question first. In this interview, Michael Howard appears to bridge at the start of his replies without dealing directly with the question.

What Mr Howard could have done instead was answer with a simple "Yes" or "No"; or alternatively replied with "I can't give a direct answer Jeremy because…" and give a persuasive reason, before then bridging to his message.

Under sustained questioning, always go back to ABCDE

In high-profile grillings in the media or at public inquiries, following the ABCDE formula meticulously during tough questioning is a way to prevent yourself being seen as a question avoider.

The formula enables you to engage with the question and still get your message across.

To take the pressure off yourself, you need to deal properly with the A part of the formula at the start – either by answering the question or by acknowledging it and immediately explaining why you can't answer it. Then and only then should you bridge to your message, say the best thing you can say and/or put the answer you've given into a broader context. To do otherwise leaves your interviewer and audience dissatisfied, as Mr Howard found.

There are particular times when I feel an overwhelming duty to tell audiences about the Howard–Paxman interview. It's whenever someone claims that the way to deal with tough questions is to ignore them and just say whatever they want – or when someone mistakenly suggests that proper media interview training involves learning to evade the question. It's all about effectively answering the question before conveying your message – in case there's any doubt!

The Howard–Paxman interview demonstrates exquisitely that avoiding the question when faced with a competent, persistent interviewer doesn't work. If you have any doubts about this, type into your search engine: "Jeremy Paxman's infamous Michael Howard interview". Watch it, then ask yourself if avoiding the key question when you're in the public spotlight is a good idea.

In tough media interviews and when at a public inquiry, answering the key question – or explaining why you can't answer it – is vital to your credibility. There are moments when it's absolutely essential to say more than what you're being asked. In these cases, getting the elements of your answer in the right order is critical to that success. The ABCDE formula allows you to achieve this.

Because of the exposure you get in situations where there is a strong public interest, what you say matters more than ever. It goes on public record and so can be closely studied at the time – and forever. Your performance can be scrutinized or the transcript read on the Internet over and over.

Ambitionwise, Mr Howard's career didn't live happily ever after following that interview.

But your story can have a happy ending. As your career unfolds and you achieve ever-greater prominence, you never know when you'll end up in the public spotlight – on radio, television or at an inquiry.

Learning from Michael Howard's experience, you'll hopefully find that with the right approach, any moments you have in the limelight can potentially tell a much happier story.

While most media interviews aren't as combative as the Howard–Paxman experience, journalists will typically pounce on a perceived flaw in an argument or highlight a weak point.

So you should always be ready for the toughest possible questions in any circumstance. Even in softer, glossy magazine-style interviews, challenging questions can lurk amidst the fluffier ones.

Getting it right in that interview request call

The first step to standing up successfully to challenging interview questions starts when the media representative approaches. Building on what was discussed in Chapter 4 about finding out in advance what's on their agenda, you need to get it right when that initial request for an interview is made…

Ring. Ring.

> *"Hello. It's XYZ Broadcasting here. Can you do an interview about your organization?"*

Do you say "Yes" or "No"? (*Warning*: Many get this wrong!)

Often people say an immediate "No", because they're excessively nervous and fear negative questioning.

However, an instant "No" can signal to the media that your organization is doing something bad – and you're trying to hide it, or hide from it. This is the impression the media often conveys to its audiences when referring on air to the decline of an interview request: "We called Company YYY about their alleged involvement in the sudden deaths and no one would comment."

An instant refusal means you could be missing out on a potentially great opportunity for generating fantastically positive exposure before a large audience. Alternatively, some people give an immediate "Yes" and by doing so agree to an encounter that they don't know enough about and without allowing themselves time to plan. This lays the groundwork for an interview car crash.

You can probably work out from this that both an immediate "Yes" and an immediate "No" to the interview request are wrong. Yet it's amazing how many otherwise streetwise people go for one or the other of these instantly incorrect choices. The right answer is to find out more before making a considered decision.

Asking the right questions, so you can prepare the right answers

The key to making the right decision involves asking the right questions.

Finding out more about what's behind the interview request is always an option, even though the news media won't always volunteer that the option is available.

Keep in mind that by approaching you, the media demonstrate that they want something from you. This gives you some power to ask polite questions of them with the realistic expectation of getting answers.

When you're live on television and the bright lights are on, you may well feel as though you have less power. Use your power before you've agreed to anything to find out more about what their thinking is behind the interview request.

True, media representatives ringing you can be under pressure not to voluntarily give too much away. They typically won't want to signal that you're in for a rough time, for fear of frightening you off. But they'll usually give you some additional information if you play things right.

My suggested starting point, without promising at this stage to do the requested interview, is to signal a general enthusiasm for helping the media outlet. But you need to discover more about the specific situation before you can sensibly decide whether doing a particular interview is right for you or your organization. So ask something simple like: "What exactly do you need from the interview?"

This is a far better approach than the crass method of asking "What are the questions going to be?" You could hardly design a response that sounds more paranoid, alarmed and guilty! It's rather like saying to someone in a high-stakes card game: "Before we start betting, can you show me what's in your hand?"

Besides, the media aren't typically going to give you an actual list of questions. Asking for more information about what's behind the request is effectively probing the same territory as "What are the questions?" But it sounds far more relaxed. It will typically earn you a more generous response and project a more composed image.

Remember, your underlying aim in this situation is to find out as much as you can about the potential interview without actually committing to doing it on the spot. If probed in the right way, the media representative may well be profoundly helpful.

A media interview itself will naturally be all about the journalist asking you questions, but in the all-important pre-interview chat you want to be the one asking most of the questions.

Tapping into the power of asking questions

One thing to be wary of – especially when dealing with radio journalists specifically – is to avoid actually allowing a telephone interview to start there and then. It's amazing how many people fall into this trap – and give off-the-top-of-their-head answers that they come to regret. By only asking questions in the preliminary chat phase, you can avoid this happening. And you can simultaneously be building your knowledge of the situation, so you're in a better position to make the right decision.

There are a number of questions you need to ask the media caller. Among them:

- "What issue are you exploring?" Or in media phraseology: "What angle are you looking at?" (This aims to ensure you're told more than just a topic, by seeking the particular aspect of the subject to be examined.)

- "What's your understanding of the story?" (Journalists often have an idea about the ultimate story they're pursuing – which eventually may prove to be true or wildly inaccurate. It's your job to at least unearth the theory they're working on.)

- "Who else are you talking to?" (This is a massively useful question. If you discover they're also interviewing your arch rival, a competitor or a group protesting about your organization, you'll gain an immediate understanding of where the questions will be coming from without specifically asking.)

- "What is your target audience?" (Ask this if you aren't familiar with the media outlet, so you know the kind of people listening. Remember, you're ultimately doing an interview for them!)

- "Would the interview be live or pre-recorded?" (Contrary to many people's misguided belief, a live interview is often the better alternative. It may seem scarier – but everything you say goes out unedited. This gives you greater control over what gets broadcast.)

Don't lull yourself into a false sense of security by mistakenly thinking that if it's pre-recorded and you say something stupid or wrong, the media will automatically be happy to cut that bit out. They may or they may not. The media take the view that they own the interview. If a bit you want removed is significant, the interviewer may need to refer upwards for a decision. This makes a bigger deal of whatever gaffe you've made.

When you've obtained all the information you require, it's often best not to give an immediate reply to the "Will you or won't you be interviewed?" question. There may be times when you can give an instant "Yes", such as when you're conducting a string of interviews on the topic, so you're already on top of the situation. However, it's usually better to buy yourself some thinking time.

A good last question is: "When do you need an answer by?" Get the journalist's telephone number and commit to a time within their deadline limits when you'll call back. Now you have the opportunity to properly decide whether you should do the interview. You also have the chance to consult colleagues – including your boss – and to consider whether you or someone else in your organization is actually best placed to do it.

You can then ring back the journalist and either decline or agree to the interview.

If you say "No" you don't have to give a reason, but it's good if you can volunteer a credible one. It's helpful to indicate that in the future you may well be able to do an interview and that they should feel free to call again on another occasion.

If you say "Yes" you can now feel so much better about the interview because you have bought time to prepare answers to the kind of questions you're well equipped to predict. However brilliant you are, you'll always be better with some focused preparation time. Now is the time to go through the AMEN preparation steps outlined in Chapter 4 as you prepare for the specific audience your messages and examples, and how you will deal with the negatives.

Being prepared for tough questions in an unfolding crisis

Your media interview planning has to move especially fast if your organization is dealing with a crisis – whether it's a share price slump, a product recall or some kind of physical disaster. If you're in an industry where there are inherent dangers – such as chemicals, pharmaceuticals or transport – then plans should be drawn up in advance for dealing with the media ahead of any potential disaster, just as there are typically contingency plans for what needs to be done physically in a range of conceivable emergencies. Dealing with the media should be a central part of those plans.

However good your systems are for communicating with your people internally, they can be hampered in a crisis. So, communicating through the media can be a vital way to get important messages across to your own team – as well as to the public – when something big has gone wrong. Your emergency plans should include identifying who, in various circumstances, should be responsible for talking with the media in the event of a major newsworthy development affecting your organization.

For the next part, we will work on the assumption that you are primarily responsible for dealing with the media during emergencies as a fire tragically sweeps through your headquarters.

From a media perspective, there are typically three phases in an unfolding crisis – each beginning with "M". If that large-scale bad thing happens involving your organization, you need to be ready for each phase: "Mayhem", "Mastermind" and "Manhunt".

1. Keeping cool during the mayhem

The mayhem stage happens when the incident first takes place. There's typically much confusion, and the media seeks to grab whatever facts and interviews they can.

In the early stages of the happening, the media will be hungry for your input. Providing you can gather enough facts to be credible, there are advantages in being interviewed early. This allows you to demonstrate a responsible attitude on behalf of your organization at the outset, in a way that would not be conveyed if you remained silent or reverted to a "no comment" approach. When you help the media in gathering material, you have a much better chance of influencing how they cover the story.

However, it's also wise to liaise with the authorities about what type of information should be revealed publicly about sensitive aspects such as any deaths. If there is bad news to announce, it needs to be done in the most compassionate way. This may be something the police or fire brigade are best suited to handle in the first instance, as they'll want to ensure, for example, that close relatives of the deceased don't hear names identified through the media first.

One thing you need to be especially careful to avoid in the mayhem stage is saying anything that will put you in the wrong position if the direction of the story suddenly changes. Be wary of saying something that could turn out to be untrue hours, days or months later. The kind of line that can be dangerous is: "Everyone in the company is safe", when it's still possible that someone may turn out not to be. So it's vital to insert brief qualifications on what you say, such as "From what we know at the moment…" or "Preliminary indications suggest…"

Be especially careful about anything you say concerning the future – which is a strangely unpredictable place. Keep in mind that in the mayhem phase, when there's limited reliable information, making predictions as part of your interview answers can be particularly dangerous.

Avoid saying something that you can't really promise, like "We guarantee that this kind of disaster will never happen again". Saying something more realistic is far preferable and more credible, such as "We will do everything we can to seek to ensure that a disaster of this kind never happens again". This could be one of your key messages.

2. Beware the dangers of speculation
The mastermind phase is where the media – having accumulated all the initial information they can get – typically run into a period

when new information is scarce. This can be when officials such as fire brigade chiefs or senior police start investigating causes and may not be able to share their findings immediately with the media. The phase is called mastermind because this is where the media typically seek out experts not involved in the immediate situation and push them to speculate about what has happened and what might happen next. If you're doing an interview in this period, beware the danger of being pushed into unwise speculation. Explain why you can't answer some questions and bridge to information you can verify.

3. Demonstrating a responsible approach during the manhunt

The third phase – the manhunt – is where the media seek to expose who is to blame (man or woman!) for whatever has gone wrong. In this phase you need to be cautious about causes – for obvious legal reasons. It can be important to obtain advice from a lawyer before a media interview so you are clear on what you can say and what you can't safely say. But having taken legal advice, remember that how you phrase things is crucial. At all times, without accepting any blame unfairly, you need to express concern for victims and their families and friends and demonstrate a responsible attitude.

If your organization is in the blame spotlight during this phase, then the "specific-to-general" approach can be very useful in order to convey points when there are still so many facts to establish. So if asked whether a specific factor is responsible for what's gone wrong, you can explain, if appropriate, that it is too early to identify anyone in particular, but move to address the question in more general terms.

If your organization is being accused through the media of being at fault, this is the time when, having dealt with the question directly, you can convey messages about how important safety is to your company – with illustrations to back this up. And it's the time to say that you're doing everything you can to assist any inquiries – assuming of course that you are. In moving from the specific to the general, it can be the time to talk about your organization's excellent safety record, your commitment to ever-higher safety standards, and how efforts will be made to learn any lessons.

In the manhunt phase it's vital to be aware of the emotions that those adversely affected by the events are experiencing. While taking reasonable steps to defend yourself and your organization, you must ensure you connect emotionally with the audience by utilizing the CARE formula, as outlined in Chapter 6, which ensures that answers address the heart before the head, and reminds you to express concern for any victims and those who care about them at the start of your first answer in any interview.

If your organization ends up being accused of wrongdoing, you naturally need to seek advice from lawyers on what can and cannot be said. But don't let this stop you being warm and compassionate. Being seen publicly to do nothing more than protect your narrow legal position can be counterproductive. Organizations that are only concerned with limiting legal damage can do enormous damage to their reputation if this prevents them being seen as caring and humane.

If your company is at the centre of a disaster and you do well with your media approach during the mayhem, mastermind and manhunt phases, your organization will typically end up having a much better public image than if you had shied away from any media exposure. This puts you in a stronger position in terms of image when it comes to dealing with any public inquiry set up in the wake of a disaster. But, however well you've done when appearing before the media, such an inquiry holds challenges of its own. Here is some guidance…

In the inquiry spotlight, say what needs to be said

By the time the media coverage gets well into the manhunt phase, some kind of health and safety or public inquiry into the disaster may be underway. Such an inquiry or inquest holds a new set of challenges for anyone or any company that's required to give evidence before it – especially for those called as witnesses in a public inquiry.

In these kinds of situations, people being questioned are often being urged by legal teams outside the inquiry and officials inside it to just answer the questions and say nothing more. While it's important to show respect to those directing proceedings and answer their questions where you can, it's vital that you don't become trapped by the limited scope of questions. Answering questions through the ABCDE formula is vital. You need to ensure that limiting questions don't stop you from getting across crucial points, which may well be in the interests of the inquiry, your organization and justice. Having your own set of messages to convey is as vital to your success in a public grilling as in any other situation.

I have on occasions teamed up with a highly experienced and enlightened lawyer-cum-trainer to run sessions guiding those who appear in legal cases as professional witnesses. This means that the witnesses don't have a direct personal involvement in the case being examined, but are called upon to give their independent views based on their expertise. They are putting their reputations on the line. My legal colleague gets particularly concerned that those giving evidence are often made to feel – by lawyers and inquiry officials – that they must only answer questions and say nothing more. We both know that witnesses can be trapped badly at times if they don't add important additional clarifying information. In order to convey his point to our forthcoming witnesses, he plays a specially made video featuring a chilling fictional – but scarily realistic – scene.

The video action takes place inside a courtroom, where a professional witness – in this case a medical doctor – takes the stand. He's giving evidence under cross-examination by a ruthless lawyer seeking to boost the case of his client by unfairly undermining the doctor's reputation. The dialogue goes something like this.

Lawyer: "Doctor, you've been the medical practitioner for some of the most prominent citizens in this town haven't you?"

Doctor (swelling with pride): "Yes, that's true."

Lawyer: "Were you the medical practitioner for the former mayor, George Smith?"

Doctor: "Yes."

Lawyer: "How is Mr Smith?"

Doctor: "He's dead."

Lawyer: "Oh. I see. Well you treated the former town clerk, John Jones, didn't you?

Doctor: "Yes."

Lawyer: "How is Mr Jones?"

Doctor: "He's dead."

Lawyer: "Oh. Now you were also the doctor for the town's former bank manager, Fred Robinson, weren't you?"

Doctor: "Yes."

Lawyer: "How is Mr Robinson?"

Doctor: "He's dead."

At this point everyone in the courtroom is looking at the doctor as if he's a mass murderer. What they don't know from the evidence is that his deceased former patients were all extremely old and died of natural causes.

My training colleague tells our participants that what the doctor should do, when he's worked out where the line of questioning is heading, is to turn to the judge and say something like: "Your Honour, the court needs to know that these men were all in their late nineties when I was treating them. They had lived long healthy lives and they all died of natural causes."

This kind of answer puts a whole new complexion on the evidence. But we would only get the full picture if the doctor took the initiative to put the situation into a proper perspective.

That's why it's important for you not to be boxed in at a public hearing to the extent that you allow yourself to be prevented from conveying important truths and vital messages.

Your role in conveying the wider picture

Sometimes direct, honest replies which only answer the immediate question cannot convey enough of the whole picture or deal with the complexities of truth. So it's vital when giving evidence that you go beyond the scope of the immediate questions, if sticking within their limitations creates a false impression. If possible it's good to explain that you are taking this extra step in the interests of helping the inquiry establish the truth. The ABCDE formula can rescue you here, with well-placed bridges such as "What everyone looking at this case needs to know is..." and "It's vital for the sake of justice to take into account..."

However many lawyers, judges and journalists you're surrounded by, your primary role is to go beyond just answering the questions and to convey necessary wider truths and important messages. If you do this well the inquiry will be grateful, although you may have to be heroically assertive at times in order to give them this assistance.

You would not want the inquiry to miss out on vital information. And like the doctor in the video, you don't want to allow yourself to be inaccurately portrayed as a serial killer when you're a wonderful, warm, loving individual who shows goodwill to all.

Your role is to convey your vital truths as well as your important messages and illustrations.

In public hearings, in the media and beyond, this is what you need to do in order to come out a winner every time.

ONGOING ENHANCEMENT: GREAT ANSWERS FOR YOUR INSPIRATIONAL FUTURE

At this concluding point, hopefully you've taken a giant leap towards becoming walking, talking, living proof of what's been maintained throughout this book – that giving great answers to tough questions in the workplace is a learnable, improvable skill.

And hopefully you've had the chance to try things out with anyone in your working world who has been asking you tough questions.

Maybe you and they have already noticed a difference in your persuasiveness and the image you project.

If not, then maybe you're about to make that amazing leap.

If you look back at that toughest question that you wrote in the box at the end of Chapter 1, it should look a lot easier to give a great answer to it now.

Hopefully you're feeling more confident about answering it with enhanced content, structure and delivery style.

And you can presumably see how – now that you have simple steps you can go through to plan great answers – you can use the same techniques to deal with other tough questions that will arise during your career. This even includes questions you and your would-be tormentors haven't yet thought about!

But however brilliant you've so far become at giving great answers, in all probability your best is still ahead of you.

Giving great answers is not just a learnable skill – it's also a skill you can constantly refine. Working on doing this should be a rewarding, career-long joy.

One thing, for example, that you should aim to progress at with further practice is utilizing the golden formulae in ways that are increasingly more subtle, sophisticated and bedazzling. For example, you can work at ensuring that your bridging with the ABCDE formula is smoother and more natural as you glide more seamlessly from one aspect of your answer to another. This means that the actual golden formulae themselves won't appear as obvious to anyone who doesn't actually know them.

Constantly regenerating your answers

You can also get to a higher level by enhancing the quality of the elements you deploy within your answers. You can improve it over time by taking out old bits and adding in new bits for different audiences. You should always seek to refresh your great answers if you're using them for more than one occasion. This is especially so with the examples and case studies that you deploy. It's desirable to update them so that your askers get the most recent ones and those that are most relevant to them.

It's also worth watching masters of the art give great answers wherever possible – and learning from them as you do so. Observing interviewing performances on news and current affairs programmes can become all the more engrossing when you're watching for who uses the formulae well and how. Also look out for whatever else they do in their answers that you can learn from.

And when you see a disaster of an answer from someone who is not so good at it, always seek to identify what it was they did incorrectly and how they could have avoided it. It's particularly useful to look at what people in your field are doing that works well.

The news media tend to gravitate towards certain spokespeople and commentators to interview over and over, so this allows you to make a point of watching closely what it is that the impressive ones are doing with their great answers. Along the way you can even be selecting who might be a good role model for you.

But when it comes to your own performances you do, of course, need to give answers in a style that is consistent with the authentic you. Be yourself. But as you plan and project your great answers, work at constantly improving that best possible version of yourself to project.

And while you should always think carefully about the questions you're likely to get – and plan answers for them ahead of time – ultimately remember that your answers are even more important than their questions. Here's a final story to remind you.

Many years ago there was a problem for the education authorities in Australia, when copies of the final high school public examination papers were stolen. What made things worse was that there were reports of some of the exam papers actually being sold to students who were about to sit the tests. I remember a front-page newspaper cartoon which featured a pupil who clearly looked as though he wasn't very bright. He was going up to someone selling the exam papers on a street corner. But what the pupil came out with showed that he wasn't as stupid as he looked. In the caption the pupil said to the seller: "I know you want fifty dollars for the *questions*. How much do you want for the *answers*?"

It profoundly underlines the point that it's not the tough questions that are so important. It's the great answers that really count. And who controls those great answers? You do, of course!

So here's wishing you all the success in the universe for that vital question-answering aspect of your career. The answers you give can play a crucial part in how well you are perceived as doing in your current position. And your answers can play a massive part in determining what your next position will be and so much more.

Whatever you do now and whatever you end up doing in the future, here's hoping you can move to a point where the answers you give are consistently great ones – for the benefit of yourself, your questioners and everyone else who is affected by them!

ABOUT THE AUTHOR

 Michael Dodd is an international speaker who empowers audiences to become inspirational communicators.

As a one-time broadcast journalist in the rough world of Australian politics, he asks volunteer audience members Aussie-style "blowtorch-on-the-belly" questions.

He then equips audiences to give the best possible answers to nightmare questions from clients, prospects, reporters, shareholders and career-critical interview panels.

Michael has had speaking engagements on six continents.

He's been awarded the "New Speaker of the Year" title by the Academy for Chief Executives.

He was a political correspondent for the Australian Broadcasting Corporation before becoming a foreign correspondent in London and Berlin.

Michael covered Eastern Europe before, during and after the anti-communist revolutions that brought down the Berlin Wall.

He became best known amongst international audiences for his newspaper reviews on Sky News and the British Broadcasting Corporation.

Michael is a fellow of the Professional Speaking Association and has been president of its vibrant London region.

ACKNOWLEDGEMENTS

And thanks to…

I had an uncle who lived an extraordinarily rugged life farming on Kangaroo Island off the coast of South Australia and beyond.

"You must write a book", we told him.

"That's something I will never do", he insisted.

Alas he kept his word.

But Uncle Bro didn't have a bunch of unstoppably enthusiastic colleagues in the professional speaking world to propel him.

I'm blessed that I do.

Without their "don't-take-'not-yet'-for-an-answer" approach, you wouldn't have got to read this book for a long time.

Speakers and authors Nicci Roscoe, Chris Merrington, Eilidh Milnes, Jane Gunn, John Cremer, Frank Furness, Nikki Owen, Philip Calvert, Phillip Khan-Panni, Rod Sloane, Barry Graham, Mark Fritz, Carole Spiers, Steve Clarke and more have been admirably persistent book-writing prodders and/or general encouragers.

Recovering-barrister-cum-author, learned friend and hilarious after dinner speaker Graham Davies, was masterly in enticing his publishers to consider this project.

294 ACKNOWLEDGEMENTS

My mentors – both multi-book authors and one-time national presidents of the Professional Speaking Association, Roger Harrop and Graham Jones – provided reservoirs of white-haired and grey-haired wisdom respectively.

Book midwife Mindy Gibbins-Klein and book guru Sue Richards presented gold nuggets on the mysterious book-producing realm.

So, too, did the American publishing legend Dan Poynter, sadly now writing in the library beyond after authoring 130 books on this planet.

Colleagues from the training world have given insights into inspiring communication – Andrew Boyd, Cedric Pulford, Michael Meech, Magnus Carter, Tina Coulsting Carter, Simon Mann, Jo Pearson, Steve Bustin, Neil Roberts, Chris Roycroft-Davies and Brenda Ellison. Leaping onto the backs of giants always helps us to see more.

Present and past chairs of the Academy for Chief Executives, Joanna and Phil Jesson, Gordon Bromley, Simon Lester, Jane Hunt, Nick Jackson and others helped me broaden the principles of media interview-response techniques to encompass great answers to tough questions from clients, prospects and more.

Business leaders from Vistage, MD2MD, Footdown, Executive Foundation, Business Leaders Group, Academy for Business Leaders and Entrepreneurs and the Scottish Institute for Business Leaders have put on events which have enabled the further development of the techniques.

Clients in public relations, particularly Fishburn Hedges (now FleishmanHillard Fishburn), Apollo Strategic Communications and

Grebot Donnelly, have rightly persuaded clients that answering tough questions superbly is vital to their ongoing success.

Teenage technical wizz Lucinda Dodd magically solved challenges when the intended manuscript and my computer clashed.

Development editor Jenny Ng and her colleagues at Capstone – always perceptive, organized and heartening – have constantly been on the reader's side, striving to ensure that every sentence is aimed at your best interests.

Inspirational Sydney teacher Rosa Kloczko – who has continued her support since her captivating geography lessons from some years back – deserves an A-plus for lifetime encouragement.

If Uncle Bro had been endowed with the people I've been surrounded by, his book would be on the shelves too.

INDEX